THE PLEASURE
OF
Their Company

A Memoir:
Adventures in Hand-Raising Orphan Fawns

By

Cynthia R. Hubbard

authorHOUSE®

AuthorHouse™
1663 Liberty Drive, Suite 200
Bloomington, IN 47403
www.authorhouse.com
Phone: 1-800-839-8640

© 2009 Cynthia R. Hubbard. All rights reserved.

No part of this book may be reproduced, stored in a retrieval system, or transmitted by any means without the written permission of the author.

First published by AuthorHouse 4/27/2009

ISBN: 978-1-4389-1192-2 (sc)

Printed in the United States of America
Bloomington, Indiana

This book is printed on acid-free paper.

Of Such

*are made true gifts from God –
beauty, brightness and blessings that endure.*

Dedication

To
Little Lone Fawn – My Mentor
John Doe – My Trooper
Baby Buck – My Fixture
Bambino – My Bravest
Van Doe – My Noblest

Your stories are those of exceptional friends, unique and treasured gifts from God, who with your quiet and unassuming natures taught me much about how to live and behave, whose presences brought a profound peace to my soul, home and little piece of land, and whose gentle ways always made my heart smile. Thank You for allowing me to enter your world a bit and walk awhile with you, for mentoring me in many life lessons, and for sharing your friendships with me. Blessings such as you do not come often, nor do the memories of you fade with your leaving.

FOREWORD and ACKNOWLEDGEMENTS

I've always had a reverence for and love of all animals, well, with the exception of what I call the "creepy-crawlies and sliders". If they wouldn't run or slither so, or dart so here and there, or pop up or out so unexpectedly, I wouldn't make tracks quite so fast myself and my blood pressure would be a whole lot more stable. Or if they stayed out of sight, and out of my house, I wouldn't have this, well, phobia. Over the years I've kept my eyes open for support groups such as Spiders Anonymous, but to no avail. I know…these critters are only doing what they were designed to do. It's just I wish they'd do it somewhere else. But I digress, and in all likelihood, this won't be the last time you read *that* phrase.

Penning the stories of these five orphan white-tail fawns, four that I hand-raised, was truly a labor of love for me. This, my first attempt at writing anything substantial, was all the easier because I loved the subjects so. For the special creatures they were, and for all they gave me, I felt they deserved a book. Having taken some notes during my time with each fawn was obviously a significant help in being able to tell their stories. There are many details however that are missing or vague, but are the best memory can provide since at the time I began writing, January 2007, it had been almost 20 years since the arrival of the first fawn. All those little memory cells in my brain are 20 years older now, [some have long-since flown the coop], and are being asked to hold now 58 years-worth of 'memorabilia'. That's a lot of memorabilia. I'd hate to see the mish-mash in *there*.

Since I didn't know first, that after the initial fawn another would follow and grow into a succession of five fawns, and second, that I would one day want to write a book about them, I didn't feel compelled to make sure my notes were clear, organized and complete. I certainly didn't feel any need to store them all in one drawer or desk, which I quickly discovered as I began to search for them. I obviously didn't feel any need to put them in any logical place either, which I found out right fast too. They were in some of the *oddest* places.

An additional prompt in writing their stories, one which worked to spur me on, is that this Spring, 2007, seemed to bring a greater number of fawns and their mamas into closer proximity than last year. Seeing or hearing the little ones especially, but the adults too, after allowing myself a bit of fun-time in observation or interaction, would propel me to the keyboard. Aside from this, in the years since my horses left, various deer and fawns have taken to using the stalls in my barn for relief from extreme weather, Winter and Summer especially, but also in other seasons.

Eventually, fawns learn to follow their mamas into the barn to get out of the noon-day sun or weather extremes of any kind. If I'm working outside in the yard, I can pretty much always count on one or more heads poking out from the barn or stall doors. A few of them are so used to me, that even when I go into the barn to drag out the riding mower, they may lazily rise to check out what I'm doing, but they then return to their cool spot under the fan. Whenever I see one or two going in or out of the barn, mid-smile I'm reminded, 'back to the keyboard'.

Another 'help' was the fact that from January until early June, 2007, I had a "frozen" shoulder, [adhesive capsulitis for you medical-ese buffs], which eliminated much of the activities I would normally do in winter, like skiing and indoor tennis. It didn't prevent me from typing, and I grew to see and even welcome my situation as a meant-to-be gift in a sense, affording me the time and opportunity to write their stories. And the only One *I* know who can coordinate the timing of such things and events is God. Not only will I most likely digress quite a few times in telling the stories of these five wonderful fawns, I will also give praise and thanks where praise and thanks are due, to God for all His help with these ventures, but above all, for allowing my path to cross with each of these beautiful little creatures. In addition to Him, there are several people I wish to thank:

Nancy P. Hubbard, a sister, sometime-employer, and Founder-President of two very successful Companies, one of which is Hubbard Marketing Group, Inc.: So much have you done and given to this project, this truly became "our" book. You gave me constant encouragement to "keep on writing", and were supportive in so many concrete ways. You spent hours poring over my manuscript, editing and proofing, and then more hours reviewing it all with me long-distance. And your generous offer of the services of your Company to help promote my book when it is published will be invaluable. I couldn't have done it without you.

Dana Hubbard Roscoe, a sister and English Major in college: You edited, proofed and provided so many helpful suggestions of phrasing and wording that made my pages much more user-friendly. You were my source for quotable quotes of famous folks, and you always had a word of encouragement that helped me keep going. You contributed to 'the cause' in so many ways, figuratively and literally. I couldn't have done it without you.

Dr. James Radcliffe, a friend, excellent Veterinarian, and my Vet of some thirty-plus years: You have taken exceptional care of my horses and dogs over these years. You were the conduit that sent me my first fawn, and from then on you were available to me 24/7 during my fawn-raising years, not only with moral support, but medical expertise and care, from John Doe's broken leg, tummy troubles and neutering, to Baby Buck's neutering, to Van Doe's last visit. I couldn't have done it without you.

Several friends, Employees of our local Zoo, and Animal Professionals, Handlers, and Experts on deer in particular: Your expertise and willingness to share your knowledge and information, provide much-needed guidance, and walk me through not only the good times but the rough spots too, with several of the fawns I raised, were a huge source of help and stability. In the toughest times, you were a great calming influence. I couldn't have done it without you.

Bob Mothersbaugh, Deer Expert who became a 'long-distance' friend, Director of the Deer Research Center at the University of Pennsylvania: You were receptive from the beginning to my calls for help -- from John Doe's leg and neutering, to Baby Buck's neutering, and to Bambino's bone problems. Your vast wealth of knowledge and expertise, and your support and guidance to me, and therefore to my Vet, were critical to the care and treatment of these different fawns' issues. If I didn't reach you when I called, you returned my calls so promptly. You were there for me roughly every 4 years, and in between, always so willing to help, even long-distance. I couldn't have done it without you.

Kathy Gorney Tagg, goat milk supplier: You had goats, and more importantly, Goat's Milk!, which you kindly kept in stock while I raised not only my first fawn but later ones as well. When I'd not paid attention and all of a sudden was running short, you and your goat girls were so agreeable and cooperative in getting another supply ready in no time. I couldn't have done it without you.

Sally Hobbs, a friend, large-hearted friend to animals, and co-surrogate fawn-mama: You were always so willing and helpful, with John Doe especially, but the others too as they came along, taking night shifts in the barn to give meds and TLC, spelling me during day shifts as well, or agreeing to be 'on call' and readily taking on-call duties. I couldn't have done it without you.

Ron Hobbs, a friend and Sally's husband: You were not only a big help with one of the fawns, i.e. driving us to pick up the very first fawn, fixing drinks and supplying pizza for dinner the night of his release, but more, shared your wife so she could help me with the fawns over the years. She, and therefore I, couldn't have done it without you.

Mary and Dick Porter, friends, friends to animals, and neighbors: You're two of the most generous folk I know, and bought those two deer feeders, one for your place and one for mine. You were always so interested in John Doe, and so willing to help. You headed our 'John Doe Neighborhood Watch Program' so we could get him neutered, and brought me sustenance while I sat with him in the 'Recovery Room'. I couldn't have done it without you.

Sarah Caldwell, Virginia Heinlein, Betty Kriebel, and Margaret Perry, outstanding elementary school teachers in the 50's and 60's, long gone but long remembered: You were top-notch educators in general, but specifically, provided solid foundations in grammar and all its elements, in composition and writing, back in the days when those subjects were still a main focus of good education, still taught in depth, and taught correctly. I couldn't have done it without you.

Mary Paull Hubbard Taylor, a sister and great help over the years with many of my animals: You were willing to step out of your comfort level, the one that isn't particularly fond of up-close-and-personal Kodak moments with large animals like horses, to literally get past them at times, and pinch-hit in bottle-feeding Baby Buck. You house-and-pet-sat with your three sons when I went on a trip for three weeks, and kept Van Doe on her feeding schedule. [to say nothing of caring for my four dogs and two horses!] I couldn't have done it without you.

Timothy Hubbard Taylor, my God-Son, and Shawn Taylor, my nephews: You were so enthusiastic and eager, and so frequently, to help feed Baby Buck, before and after his release, or hang with him in his stall or my yard, that it gave me time to do a few other things, like take care of my dogs and horses, clean my house, or go to market to get people-food! When your Mother and you 3 brothers house-sat, you were a great help in caring for and feeding all my critters, but especially Van Doe. I couldn't have done it without you.

Benjamin Walker Taylor, a real animal lover and my nephew: You were in there pitching, despite your young age of just three in 1999, when your Mother, you and your brothers house-sat for me, and cared for and fed all my animals, including Van Doe. In the years following, many times you helped me get Van Doe's food bowl ready and then helped me give it to her. You used to giggle so when she would walk right up on my deck. I couldn't have done it without you.

Hoon Choi, Graphics Designer Extraordinaire, and a new friend I have not yet met: Your creativity and talents brought so much to my book's presentation, with its wonderful front and back covers and distinctive section pages. Your flexibility and patience working with me over the Internet was greatly appreciated. I couldn't have done it without you.

Dr. Karl Yurko, another local Vet with expertise in several areas: You graciously jumped right in when Bambino needed a Vet and my regular one was out of town. You provided much-needed guidance and support, your Veterinary skills, time and advice, and went the extra mile more than once. I couldn't have done it without you.

Last but certainly not least, Giggy Paull Lezra, friend, cousin, and an author in her own right, "The Cat, The Hat and The Miracle" [Athenum 1967], and "Mechido, Aziza, and Ahmed" [Athenum 1969] -- if you've not read them, treat yourself to their wonder: You were a great source of encouragement to me twenty years ago when I was only toying with the idea of writing just one fawn's story, and are again now in 2007 when I returned to the idea, expanded into all my fawns' stories, and sent you rough drafts of the first pages and then the entire book. Your willingness to look over my work with the critical eyes of one experienced and published, to offer suggestions, tips and wise words of advice, and to do some editing, have been invaluable. I couldn't have done it without you.

A diverse group of folks then, you all played various parts in these stories about my fawns, and share one common and vital element -- I couldn't have done it without you. Thanks Much to you one and all.

PROLOGUE

I could not have known at the time that something good, that would span 16 years, would come from an experience heart-wrenching to me and fatal to a doe. It was however a harbinger of things to come. The certainty of this has come to me over time, and been so reinforced that there is no doubt in my mind of the connection. On a quiet Fall day in 1987, one suddenly disturbed by destruction and sadness, came the beginning of God's gift of deer into my life.

I was driving on a country road, and as many 'country folk' do, I was traveling fast. It was a blue-sky day on the open road, you know, the kind of day and road where, when the tunes on the radio are just so, you clip along to the music and all is right with the world. As I came around a corner, with a nearly-vertical bank on the left of the road and a creek on the right, a doe suddenly leapt from the creek side into the path of my car. I laid on the horn, hit the brakes hard, and panic-swerved as fast as I could to the other lane on the bank-side of the road. As luck would have it, there was no on-coming traffic. The doe continued to cross the road which I couldn't understand, and was once again right in front of my car. Why didn't she turn and go back the way she'd come, the way a deer would normally do?

I swerved back into my lane to dodge her again, still pushing hard on the brakes, astounded that in this impromptu juggling of car and deer, this pas-de-deux so badly choreographed, we'd managed to miss again. I heaved a sigh of relief as I caught a glimpse of her beginning to ascend the bank. Still swerving and braking, I came back into my lane, when out came another doe, obviously attempting to follow her friend. It was this second doe coming behind that drove the first doe to continue across -- the first making room for her friend to cross, the second making a retreat by the first impossible.

The impact was jolting and sickening, the sound of breaking glass, crunching metal, squealing tires, and the horrible thud of her body hitting my car. She had kept moving toward the bank though, so I was hopeful she was only stunned. My car finally ground to a stop and I got out.

By this time the doe was lying down along the roadside and I began to approach her. Her friend had stopped mid-ascent on the vertical bank and was looking down at us, meeting my eyes only briefly, but staring long at her friend, who was looking up at her. I had a sense that she was torn between continuing to higher safety, and a loyalty to her friend to come back to help. She started and stopped three times, looking down at her friend each time. What passed between the two, in a realm we humans can't understand, I don't know, but I know something did. After a third pause and long gaze at her friend, she disappeared from sight.

The fallen deer was conscious and watching me as I slowly knelt beside her. She did not attempt to move. A hundred yards or so up the road was a run-down bar, hopefully with a phone. I raced to it, found a phone, and called my Vet. After some pertinent questions, he presented the realities to me, the probabilities of internal damage plus fractures, and said that if when I returned to her she was still in the same position, in all likelihood there were fatal injuries. He also presented the reality that even if he could take her to his animal hospital and operate, and even if I had somewhere secure and safe where she could recuperate, she was a wild animal who would protest being cooped up, and recovery would be iffy at best. He is one of the kindest, most compassionate of Vets, and his words and tone reflected this, but the probable reality was hard to hear.

I held out hope that when I returned to the scene the doe might have risen and be shaking off the stunning she'd received. That was not the case. She was still lying there, in the same spot, her head lowered now and resting on her foreleg. I had never had an encounter with a deer, much less talked to one, let alone one I had just hit with my car, but I sat beside her and began to talk to her.

Still she did not move, confirming to me she must be badly injured. I told her how very sorry I was and began patting and stroking her neck and the side of her face. She watched me calmly as if she knew I had not meant to hurt her and would not hurt her now. There was what I can only describe as a humble look of acceptance that I can still see today. Her eyes closed a bit and I told her I hoped she was not in terrible pain. I prayed for her, and against pain. Her eyes closed fully so I patted her one last time, said a quiet goodbye and told her I was going for help. I took one last look back at her, to see if perhaps she was rallying and there was hope after all. She did not move.

I went back to the bar and phoned the Conservation Officer, dreading what had to be done but knowing that she had to be put out of her misery. It was a Sheriff's Deputy who came, in about ten minutes. Though it was barely drivable, I had pulled my car up to the bar, and pointed to where the doe was lying. I asked him to give me a few minutes to get inside the bar where hopefully the noise of the gun wouldn't reach. He kindly afforded me that, but the report carried through the walls, invading my ears and pounding me emotionally as I heard death come to this gentle doe.

When it was over, he said someone would come for her. We did the mundane things needed after an accident, like filling out reports, and called a tow truck. After getting a rental car, I finally got home, the home I was in the process of building, physically and emotionally spent. Fortunately it was quitting time so the workmen were leaving. All I wanted was peace and quiet in the grief I was feeling.

I remember lying down on the couch, crying again, and it struck me that the moments at the doe's side were remarkable, in a bittersweet way. She accepted my attempts to soothe her, her eyes reflecting only kindness, calm, and a graciousness that belied the dreadful harm that had come to her. We had been thrown together literally, and had been made friends for the briefest of moments. In those heart-breaking moments, were the seeds of wonderful experiences to come with the orphaned fawns that were to come into my life.

Their stories and our times together have their origins with her. And as I've watched the deer come through here over the years, roaming the fields or hanging around the house, bringing their young here, and as I've raised the orphans, it's never been without a thought of the beautiful doe so graceful in pain, who despite what I'd caused her had for a moment accepted me as a friend.

Part I
Little Lone Fawn – My Mentor

Chapter 1

Little Lone Fawn's story begins May 13, 1988, about six months after the accident with the doe. Looking out my kitchen window I was seeing a 'something' in the field behind my house.

At first it looked like a brown paper bag the wind had blown in. Little white flecks were all over it. I was stumped. Then the paper bag seemed to inflate, and as it grew, I saw two super-sized ears, atop a small graceful head with large soft brown eyes and a very dark nose, a fluffy brown coat with a million spots wrapped around a little body, and four legs that went on and on as they unfolded -- it was a small fawn! It was so fragile-looking I thought it must be a little girl. I have since learned that all fawns look fragile and dainty, girls and boys alike. As the days passed, I saw it was indeed a little girl.

She did a bit of stretching, surveyed her surroundings, moved a few feet further into the field, and lay down again. Lying in the tall grass beyond my back yard, she was barely visible, not only because she was small, but due to all those spots. And of course, that's how she was designed, to fade into the background and be hidden from predators.

I watched on and off from a distance that first day, waiting to see her mama come, to nurse or check on her, but none came that I saw. The next morning she was still in the tall grass but in a new spot, so surely her mama had come overnight and led her to a fresh bed.

I'm going to digress here a bit, [didn't I tell you I would?], to explain a little about fawns. They are born without a scent, making them undetectable by predators. Along with their speckled coats that camouflage them, it's a double-whammy of protection. The mama spends about four to six hours with her fawn immediately after birth, to clean and nurse it, and destroy surrounding vegetation to eliminate evidence of newborns.

The mama then leaves the fawn so her scent doesn't attract predators. The fawn spends most of its first two weeks of life alone, without mama. Whenever mama does return, she instinctively knows to stay just long enough to nurse and care for her little one. Before leaving, she leads the fawn to a new bedding and hiding spot.

Newborns nurse almost immediately, while mama is still lying on her side after delivery. This initial nursing time is essential for bonding and imprinting, especially from the mama to the fawn. The imprinting from fawn to mama takes a little longer, about two weeks, so in these first two weeks the fawn is at risk of being attracted to any larger moving object, be it dog, human, coyote, or car.

After this approximate two-week period of living basically on its own, except for brief visits from mama, the fawn will be developed enough and stronger enough not only to follow along with mama, but to flee from any potential dangers or predators. By eight weeks fawns spend half their time traveling, feeding and bedding with mama. Like her they are most active at dawn, dusk and night-time.

Back to our story. Throughout the next day as I came and went from home, I checked to see if she was there, keeping an eye out for mama. For three days she stayed in the field, moving to different spots, and there was no sign of mama. At that point I thought it fairly certain she was not just alone, but on her own, an orphan for whatever reason. It was then I named her Little Lone Fawn. So began my adventure with this fawn, who worked her way not just into my yard but into my heart.

On the fifth day she was up and about, meandering in the field. She was grazing -- or 'browsing' which I learned is the correct term. She seemed to be thriving fairly well; it looked like she'd grown a bit. In the afternoon she took up a spot in the tall grass, resting and basking in the warm sun.

I took that opportunity to bask as well, in the back yard about fifty feet from her. She watched me intently, but didn't move from her spot. Over the next half hour I crept closer and closer, pretending I was inspecting the lawn, not making eye contact. I would sneak a peek at her and we began to have eye contact. I started talking in a very quiet voice, about the weather, the day, how cute she was, and finally introduced myself.

Her time here led me to seek information on fawns, as I knew virtually nothing. I got books from the library, and contacted a few friends who worked at our local Zoo that has a deer pen. Thankfully their specialty and expertise was deer. I spent hours in the deer pen observing, which always led to more questions, and I'd seek out the experts or go back to the books. The information I gleaned started me on the path of learning about deer and fawns, a path that would become wider and more involved than I ever could have imagined.

It helped me in my understanding about Little Lone Fawn -- how and why she might have been left on her own, her growing patterns, estimating her age from her size, eating habits and food stuffs I could put out that might help her thrive even more, what to expect as she grew, and much more. The Zoo folks estimated from my description that she was around three to four weeks old. Based on that, they were able to advise me about food and amounts I could try to give her.

Chapter 2

In hindsight, I came to realize that when I first moved into the house I'd built on this hill in the country, I only saw a deer or two, and only now and then. It was Fall when I moved in, so naturally there were no spotted fawns to see, as any born that year would have already lost their spots, and the next batch wouldn't arrive until Spring.

I have to digress again here, to February 1988, three months before Little Lone Fawn's appearance, when another hint of things to come occurred. I had to put my first dog Mandy, sixteen-plus years old, to sleep, which was terribly hard. I'd raised her from a seven-week old puppy and she'd lived in five different places with me.

We had a very close relationship. We used to play hide-and-seek which should give you an insight into our relationship. She always found me sooner than I found her, but then she always had help, from whoever happened to be around when we decided to play, in finding the best hiding spots.

It was a cold snowy day. I was watching for the Vet to arrive, [the same one you'll meet throughout the fawns' stories], and just before he arrived, a group of eleven deer came up along the edge of my driveway. They went to just the edge of the woods about fifty feet from the drive, and all lay down in the open facing my house.

After it was over, my Vet carried Mandy to the grave I'd dug, then he left and I buried her. I kept glancing over at the deer that were still in their spots, the snow still falling on them. Not until after I finished burying Mandy and headed into the house did the deer get up, as a group, and slowly walk into the woods where they were shielded from the snow. Their presence seemed extraordinary to me.

As I said, there weren't many deer up here when I first moved in, that I saw anyway. I felt that this group was one of special envoys, sent to watch over my house, Mandy, and me. Their presence, the very fact that they had appeared, sat out in the snowfall through the whole event and left only after I was back inside, seemed conclusive-enough proof to me that they'd indeed been sent on an errand. They definitely helped me feel a peace and comfort at a time that was very sad. Messengers bringing such things come, I believe, from the only One able to cause such things to occur -- God.

Then Little Lone Fawn showed up a few months later, and more and more deer began appearing here routinely. It was as if her arrival here heralded the coming of all the deer who came to be my 'regulars', of which she was the first. It was interesting to watch the interplay, or not, between the other deer and Lone Fawn. She was like the "welcome wagon", outgoing, trying to greet them and make friendly overtures. They however did not return the interest. I felt sorry for her and each day was one of anticipation that perhaps this would be the day that one of the does would take pity on her.

As I came to learn, they most likely had birthed their own fawns recently, sheltered not far from here, to whom they'd be returning later, and that like most new mothers, they had their hands full. Or, they'd not yet delivered but instinctively knew their time was soon, so were building up their bodies in preparation for the nursing ahead and had no time for a foundling fawn. Either way, Lone Fawn didn't fit in with their agendas.

Each day I spent time moving closer to her, trying to find the nearest proximity just short of too close where she'd bolt. One afternoon toward the end of May I got to within three feet of her as she lay sunning herself. She was used to my voice by then, and my awkward sidling along in the grass to the edge of the field. For about a week I had been delivering apples, carrots, and grapes to her spots in the field.

I inched forward, treats in hand, and laid them below her head, not knowing if she would eat with me so close. She began to nibble eagerly. I left my hand on the ground near where I'd laid the treats, and when she took a break I slowly reached out and stroked her neck and side of her face. Amazingly she didn't flinch or bolt.

She just looked calmly at me. It was one of the sweetest moments. And in that moment, I was taken back to a country roadside and a noble doe that had let me stroke her face and neck. Chills ran up and down my spine, and several thoughts clamored for attention all at once. Had that doe left behind a fawn who became an orphan? If so, what had happened to it? Could this be hers? Was that a link here? Was there a link at all? Was I being given the chance somehow to make up for the pain and death I'd caused another deer? Would this little one remain here so I could somehow help her grow up?

I pushed aside all the questions, and decided just to enjoy the time with the fawn. I continued to sit beside her, patting and talking to her. She was content to nibble on the goodies I'd brought, or look around the field. She liked watching the birds flit by, diving into the fields after whatever it was they were after. Her head would bob as she followed their flight paths. Then she'd nibble some more. Squirrels would run in the yard or leap from tree to tree and she would watch them. She was obviously interested in the world around her. After about half an hour I thanked her for trusting me, for the nice time we had, slowly got up and went inside.

Chapter 3

The next morning there she was browsing in the field. Not far away was a doe and with her, to my excitement, two fawns! They were about the same size as Lone Fawn, so perhaps close to her age. One was lying near mama; the other was glued to mama's side, occasionally nursing, and mimicking her activity of browsing. This little group became a daily scene in my back field, and Lone Fawn made her overtures to them, especially the fawns.

There were days when I was filled with great encouragement as the three fawns would romp and play with one another, and the doe took it in stride. There were days when she was ignored or rebuffed, and my heart sank. Some days when they left, Lone Fawn would follow behind at a distance. If they stopped and glanced back at her, she'd stop dead without a look at them, drop her head and pretend to just be browsing nearby. Who says animals are "dumb"?

My encounters with Lone Fawn continued daily, taking treats to her and her becoming more and more used to me. I always called her by name and talked to her. To say it was unusual to come home to not just my pet dogs and horses, but to what seemed like my near-pet fawn, is an understatement. It was amazing to me. Some days she would be in the front yard or in the field just below it, or the pasture below the barn, or the field behind the house. I never knew where I'd find her, but I knew where to look.

As the doe and her fawns continued their visits to the back field, Lone Fawn always greeted them and tried to interact. One afternoon toward the beginning of August I was sitting in the field with Lone

Fawn when they arrived. I whispered to her that maybe today would be the day she'd be welcomed into their group. I patted her and said I'd see her later, stepping out of the scene to let nature take its course. As I walked to the house, I prayed this really would be the day.

And some times things do have a way of taking care of themselves. An hour or so later, as I watched from my deck, the crew headed off into the woods, with Lone Fawn among them, not just straggling behind, but right with the bunch, with the doe and fawns actually paying attention to her, interacting with her. My heart soared for her.

She continued to return daily, with only a few exceptions. Sometimes she was on her own, sometimes with the doe and fawns. Everyone seemed to be getting along wonderfully. About mid-August I noticed a large handsome buck, with a beautiful set of antlers, accompanying the doe and her fawns, and their now quasi-adopted sibling Lone Fawn. They certainly looked like a family, extended perhaps, but still a family - - in photo below from left to right are the 2 fawns, 'Papa', Mama and Lone Fawn on far right.

There was something wonderful in seeing this 'family', who had taken in Lone Fawn, traveling together. And now mama had apparently attracted a suitor, or maybe just a male friend. Whatever his role, he completed the family portrait. Since he couldn't have known that Lone Fawn was an adoptee, and I don't know that it would have mattered to him had he known, he treated her the same as the other fawns, which was always tolerant and friendly, with the 'settle-down kids' attitudes fathers and/or father-figures must occasionally apply.

Inevitably one of the fawns would try to engage him in play, with the characteristic hop straight up in the air, with head lowered, much like a rodeo bucking bronco does. This is deer-speak for 'wanna play?', and is very similar to that of a dog or puppy. He often responded with his own more subdued buck, and the play-jousting would begin. He took care that his antlers didn't make body contact with a fawn, and I never once saw his antlers touch them. He usually tired of the game long before the fawns, and would communicate that enough was enough. Usually he just stopped interacting and they got the message. Like most kids, they'd go find something else to occupy their time.

By this time, I often saw Lone Fawn and the other fawns playing with each other. The energy they expended and the agility they exhibited was always something astounding to witness. They raced around, chasing each other, hopping up and down or sideways at the last minute to avoid collision, making huge leaps across the fields as they darted in and out of the other deer. Play is not only important socially among deer and fawns, but is important in building up muscles and stamina.

Lone Fawn and her 'family' came here routinely. Each time I witnessed it, it was just as heartwarming as the time before. There were days that they left, and she would stay for a couple of hours. She would follow me around to whatever chore I was working on, lie down and rest near me. Sometimes I would follow her around, and sit beside her when she lay down. If someone had said to me that April that soon there would be a little fawn who would pal around with me and I with her, I'd have said, 'hmmm, time to get back on your meds don'tcha think?'

And there were days when she came in on her own, and stayed for hours. Her family may have been nearby, just not visible. If I was working in my flower beds, she would often lie in the front yard only about five feet away. I never knew her to eat any of my flowers which was true of every orphaned fawn I raised, with one small exception of a few dogwood leaves which you'll read about later.

Other days she would leave when her family left, or if they got a bit of a head start, she would race to catch up, with those exuberant leaps that are fawns' signatures, that seem to shout "Joy to the World!" There were other days when some signal, unseen by me, that obviously meant 'time to go', passed from mama or the buck to the fawns, including Lone Fawn, because all of a sudden, and as a group, they stopped whatever they were doing and left together.

Chapter 4

Generally it appeared that the family allowed her to come and go from them as she chose. She seemed to know she had her place with them as and when she chose, and knew as well that she had a place here and with me. She was able to walk both worlds, and was welcome in both. This walking both worlds, deer and human, would be true of every fawn I raised.

It was always something that, in reflection, I found rather extra-remarkable with Lone Fawn. I'd not raised her, so there wasn't the initial bonding and imprinting that occurs naturally with bottle-feeding and all the rest that goes along with hand-raising orphan fawns. I think perhaps I just happened along at a time when she needed a friend, not to feel so alone, and that this served as the bond.

The mortality rate of fawns in general is high, orphaned fawns higher still. The fact that Lone Fawn was an orphan, and yet had survived and thrived so well, made her one of those statistics that defies the odds. That our paths crossed and I was able to supplement her diet, perhaps did make the difference at a critical point in her life.

I should mention that I never stopped greeting and talking to her, and that I continued to give her treats of apples, carrots and grapes whenever the opportunity presented itself, which it did at some point most every day as she was here most every day. The family would eye us, but never intrude or interrupt. The two fawns would venture closer to investigate just what their friend was doing so close to this stranger, but the minute I would speak to them they would bolt back to mama and the buck as fast as their legs would carry them.

It always made me chuckle, as Lone Fawn would remain calm and keep eating.

Summer days rolled by. The beginning of September Lone Fawn began to lose her spots. The ones that remained took on a ragged appearance, their whiteness and shape becoming blurred. As the spots faded and disappeared, her coat became sleeker and began turning the gray-brown typical of deer coats in Fall.

We would often stroll into the woods, on or off the beaten paths of the deer. I tried to remember to always have my camera handy, and she never seemed to mind the 'photo ops'. Her ears remained her outstanding feature and made her easily and instantly recognizable. Even as her spots disappeared entirely and she resembled other young deer, her ears practically called to me saying 'it's me'.

When the doe, buck and fawns, plus other deer, were in the field, if Lone Fawn was there, I could pick her out right away. And her face always had that sweet expression.

With the increase in deer, I had put out three salt licks that became popular spots with the deer. At some point too I began buying extra horse feed, in fifty-pound bags. At the height of consumption I went through, or rather the deer went through two hundred fifty to three hundred pounds of feed a week. I just went through a lot of money. But I'd learned that especially during Winter, or nursing times for does, they needed all the extra sustenance they could get, so I was glad to provide nourishment for them. Grain, especially sweet feed with the molasses, helps them stay warm, just as it does for horses.

Just beyond my driveway toward the woods was a main thoroughfare of the deer. I made it the main feeding station, my version of the "Circle of Life", where I would pour out fifteen to twenty piles of grain from a bucket three times a day. Much like the mailman, 'neither rain, nor sleet nor dark of night...' kept me from feeding them. It didn't take long before the deer associated the sound of grain sliding over tin with breakfast-lunch-or-dinner-time, and within minutes, sometimes seconds, there would be from two to twenty deer gathered peacefully around the feeding circle, all munching away, enjoying the meal.

I sometimes had not finished pouring out the bucket before one or two would already have taken up a spot on the circle and be eating, and as I moved around the circle pouring out piles of grain, deer would be filling up the circle behind me. There were days too when deer seemed to just materialize before my eyes, out of nowhere. They are such quiet souls; they could be lying nearby and not be noticed among the vegetation. And when they walk they hardly make a sound, so I often didn't hear them as they came to the circle. I'd look up and there they'd be. They didn't seem to mind my presence, although I would back away when I finished pouring and as the circle became fully occupied.

If Lone Fawn happened to be there by herself I could stay, as I could with the fawns I raised. But the wild ones would only tolerate so much of my closeness, and I respected that and moved away quietly. On cold snowy days, and days when winds were brutal, it made me feel good to see the deer at the circle knowing the grain would help them stay warm. For 16 years I supplied grain 3 times a day at the feeding circle. It was a joy to watch them all come and fill their stomachs.

Of course, with the fawns I raised, their dining spots were not just the feeding circle, but anywhere and everywhere around my house and property, with individual bowls and extra-special treats. Many were the days when I gazed out a window and there was one of my fawns gazing in, sometimes just on the other side of the window. No shrinking violets were they. I would learn later that fawns and deer can and will climb a couple of steps, and are not averse to walking on decks.

Chapter 5

Winter arrived early that year. November 10 brought the first snowfall. I saw the buck and mama and two fawns come up the path along the driveway and go over to the salt lick. They stayed for a few minutes then moved off into the woods. Five minutes later, up the same path came Lone Fawn. This was her first snow and she seemed to be taking it in stride. She went to the salt lick and worked at it for about five minutes.

Occasionally she would look around, taking in the new look to the scenery, then return to licking. I noticed some movement behind the salt lick, in the trees about thirty feet behind her. Through my binoculars I saw it was the doe, the mama, who had returned and lay down facing her. It seemed to me that she had come back to make sure Lone Fawn was coming along behind them, and when she saw her still at the lick, decided to stay and watch over her.

She stayed there for about five minutes, then slowly got up and headed back the direction she and the buck and fawns had gone some minutes earlier. Lone Fawn seemed totally unaware that the doe had come, or that she lay down behind the salt lick. Nor did she seem to take note when the doe got up and headed further into the woods. At least she never raised her head or looked in that direction.

The doe disappeared into the woods. No more than one minute later, Lone Fawn turned, headed to the exact spot where the doe had been lying, and then followed the same path the doe had taken. In the following photo, you can just make out the doe lying down in the upper left background.

Through the rest of November we had our usual amount of snowfall. The feeding circle was full every day, three times a day. Lone Fawn was there at least twice a day, most days three times, and some days four times. She also came over to the house for her bowl of treats from me at least a couple times daily. She had filled out well, and increased her body fat which is crucial for a fawn if it's going to survive its first winter. Her coat was thick which would also help keep out the cold.

Storing fat in the Fall is a mechanism that enhances survival during Winter months, as the fat reserves can be metabolized for energy needs when forage is sparse. It is crucial for fawns to accumulate body bulk, weight, and fat, and to be at their full potential growth heading into Winter, although they may not reach this until December. Lone

Fawn looked particularly fit when Winter came, which would be of great benefit to her, and which gave me great hope for her survival. This was borne out when Spring arrived and she had indeed come through Winter just fine.

If you've never gotten to pat a deer in wintertime, you're missing one of nature's real surprises. Their hair follicles are hollow, designed to puff up to keep out the cold. I didn't get to test it on Lone Fawn, as she never let me get that 'hands-on' with her, but was able to with two of the fawns I raised. On the coldest, snowiest, windiest day, you can put your hand down through their hair and coat, lay it against their body, and what you will find is toasty warm.

There were many days that Winter when I could tell her coat was doing its thing and keeping her warm. The first time I saw this up close though, with her hair all poofed out, I thought she was having an allergic reaction to something. A call to my deer expert friends explained it, and I was relieved. It's just one more clever design of God's that protects the deer.

Into December and the beginning of January the snows continued. Lone Fawn kept coming daily, with her family, or just ahead of or behind them. She and they always went to the feeding circle, and she always came over to the house for her treats.

Had I known that in four months I would be raising my first orphaned fawn, I might have kept taking more photos and notes about Lone Fawn. As I didn't know though, my photo record of her ends with the one above, taken January 8, 1989. The photo isn't very clear as it's taken through my dining room window and there's a reflection. But if you look closely, you can see that her coat is all puffed up, and it's especially noticeable on her face. So I know she was toasty warm that day. She is just off my deck, waiting patiently for her bowl of treats. Her family was across the drive at the feeding circle. She had her bowl and walked over to rejoin them. Then the five of them walked into the woods.

She was here through the rest of January, through February, and I saw her when Spring arrived. But beyond that I can't remember, nor did I make note of the last time I saw her, or the last time she came for her treats. If it is true that to every thing there is a season, she and I had three seasons together -- Summer, Fall, and Winter -- and with the arrival of Spring, she had other paths to take, as did I.

My times with her were very special. She was the first fawn with whom I'd ever had any interactions or relationship. Tolerant of me, befriending me, she opened up a whole new world to me, taught me so much about fawns and deer, my mentor -- Little Lone Fawn.

She helped prepare me for what was to come. What came was not only an orphaned fawn, but an injured orphaned fawn. I was going to need every scrap of information I'd gleaned about fawns, and deer in general, plus a whole lot more.

Part II
John Doe – My Trooper

Chapter 1

What else do you name a baby male deer whose identity and parentage are not known? John Doe, of course. That seemed a no-brainer. His mama had been killed by a car and a passing motorist noticed him nearby, picked him up, and took him to a Veterinarian's office. She carried the little fawn wrapped in a blanket into the office, said she was going to park her car and would be right back. She might just as well have said "the check's in the mail", as that's the last she was seen.

As 'fate' would have it, this was at my Vet's, whom I'd called the day I'd hit the doe many months before. Shortly after the fawn's arrival he called me, saying he had an orphaned male fawn, with a "bum leg", that needed some "TLC", and would I be interested and willing to be his surrogate mama, house him in my barn and raise him? It sounded like fun to me.

I didn't take time for mundane questions like, how bum IS his leg or what exactly does TLC mean? but enlisted a friend to help me pick up the little guy. She enlisted her husband to drive, so we three recruits toodled off to the Vet's, picked up the fawn, along with some advice on feedings and being a surrogate mama. I took time *then* to ask for more specifics, and that's when we got into nipple and bottle sizes, daily requirement of 32 oz of goat milk he would need, 8 oz roughly every four hours more or less, bathroom habits for which 'mama' has to provide hands-on help to get things rolling, and the eventual need to address the issue of his bad leg, which it seemed might be broken, "to some degree".

To, "it sounded like fun to me", was added "I think I need a bigger boat." And to that I added that well-thought-out ecclesiastical prayer,

"Oh God HELP!" First things first, we needed to get him to my barn, fix it up so he was safe, secure and comfy. I needed to explain to my horses, Elmo and Ebony, that not only would they be sharing the barn but the other stall too for awhile whenever they were inside, as we had a guest who would be occupying the first stall. Then I just needed to find a goat. Simple enough.

The ride home was fairly uneventful except for his thrashing around. Apparently we had reached his limit of sitting still or being contained in a blanket. In fact, we reached that limit when we still had fifteen minutes drive left, and he had no trouble getting that message across to me. I was shocked at how much wallop a little hoof could deliver. My thighs were bruised after the journey, but it was a good lesson as I learned I needed to wear long jeans not shorts, until his patience wasn't being tried and we got better acquainted. I was still sore the next day.

I carried him into the barn, and set him down in the first stall. He poked around here and there, spent some time just looking at us, and didn't mind our moving around him, talking, and patting him. He was calm, accepting of us and his new surroundings.

So that hot summer day June 24, 1989, John Doe was ensconced in my barn, with piles of fresh sawdust and hay pushed around into a wonderfully cushy full-stall bed. He made himself right at home.

He could walk fairly well despite something obviously wrong with his front left leg. It definitely stuck out near his knee, although he was able to put some weight on it to get around. He didn't complain vocally, so it didn't seem he was in any pain. For all he had been through, and for all he was yet to experience, from the start he was a great little trooper.

My Vet suggested I contact the Department of Wildlife of our state, to get an ok on raising a fawn, as it was basically illegal to do so without one. I was hesitant, wondering what I would do if they said I was not allowed. But that afternoon, I called our local Conservation Officer. He happened to have known my Father and said he would put in a good word for me with the Wildlife Department. He must have done so, as when I contacted them, after just a few perfunctory questions, I was an authorized Wildlife Rehabilitator. No courses, no pre-requisites for the non-existent courses, no exams, no awards banquet, no graduation ceremony, no caps and gowns, no nothin'. Just 'Poof-you're a Wildlife Rehabilitator'. Obviously I would be part of the "Learn as You Go" program.

This is a good time to mention something very important, a caution and word to the wise. Often, much too often, but out of the goodness of their hearts, folks "rescue" an "abandoned" fawn. In reality, and more often than not, the fawn is not abandoned, and not only does its "rescue" become detrimental and potentially lethal or fatal to the fawn's health and survival, it breaks up a family. The mama will look for days for its fawn; if you're around, you'll hear her doing her grunt-rumble unhappy sound.

If one successfully captures the fawn, but isn't able to care for it or find someone who will, and after twelve hours or so tries to return it to its spot, the mama may have since moved on. Even if reunited with its little one, it may reject the fawn because of the human smells now on it. Then the fawn truly will be abandoned. It will bleat for days, missing and searching for its mama, and wander around disoriented, miserable, and most likely starving, prey for anything that comes along, cars, dogs, or coyote.

Granted, there are Wildlife Rehabilitators available in different states, but it is not always within viable traveling distance. Folks then try to raise the fawn on their own, which may be successful in varying degrees, but then comes the dilemma of what to do with it when it's old enough to be on its own. If they have a Vet and deer expert to guide them, and happen to live near some woods where it's safe to release it, things may work out fine. Often though, those aren't available and folks then try to keep it as a pet, which is a bad situation for the deer mainly, but also for the hand-raisers as you'll later read.

In general, mamas leave their fawns for long, long hours, with explicit instructions to their little ones in 'mama-deer-speak', to stay in that spot, and wait for mama to come back. There is no hard and fast rule for how long an individual mama may leave its fawn unattended. While folks may think they watch non-stop for the mama to return, they undoubtedly may miss those times and come to a wrong conclusion that mama never returned. Admittedly there are cases when a fawn has been truly abandoned. Its mama may have been killed by a car or predator, or other incident, even during delivery. Such cases require rescue. Or, the fawn may be deformed, injured or sickly, and as cruel as it sounds the mama does abandon such a fawn. This presents a particularly difficult problem and a Vet, Game Warden or Zoo official is needed to intercede.

In any situation, I don't dare prescribe any time frame for making a decision on when to "rescue" a fawn. I will only say that, short of observing evidence of blood or bones sticking out, or an emaciated or very sickly state, any of which require immediate medical help, its far better to err on the side of leaving a fawn just where you find or see it, for at least three days before even talking with a professional for advice. In other words, don't rush to "rescue". Now, back to our story.

Chapter 2

While John Doe was settling in, I went to get supplies: baby bottles and nipples, cotton balls, and goat's milk. Thanks to one of the Zoo folks, a source of fresh goat's milk was found. A girl just a few minutes farther out in the country had goats, and voila! Goat's milk!

My friends had stayed behind to watch over the new arrival, and the horses, whose curiosity was growing at what was behind the now-closed Dutch doors leading from the run-in shed to the stalls. Actually their curiosity was minimal compared to their being miffed at being blocked out of their stalls. When I returned, my friend's husband was sitting outside the barn near the horses, and my friend was in the stall making up with John Doe who was actually lying down resting. This friend was to become increasingly invaluable as the days progressed, generously taking late-night, through-the-night or early-morning feedings, or supervising in general so I could get some rest. Since she'll be mentioned often, let me introduce Sally.

Time came to see if he was hungry enough to accept me feeding him milk from a bottle, and goat's milk at that. I hoped I didn't have a discriminating little gourmet fawn on my hands that would turn up his nose at anything but mama's milk, and directly from mama. Fortunately he dove right in, eagerly, hungrily, and as if he'd been drinking from a bottle all his life.

That first day, I guesstimated his weight to be around fifteen to twenty pounds, more or less. The deer experts at our Zoo gave me a feeding schedule with appropriate amounts for his estimated weight, from which they also figured him to be about three or four weeks old. Ideally he should have four bottles a day, with no more than eight and no less than five ounces at a time. If this initial feeding with him being so exuberant a drinker was any indication, it seemed this would be no problem. Indeed it was no problem. He would take eight ounces at a clip, or most of it, the required four times a day. I did weigh him on June 26 and he was twenty-five pounds, so he'd either gained ten or five pounds roughly, or I'd over or under estimated his weight. Either way, he was definitely thriving.

The four times a day usually began around 7 am, then 11:30-ish, late afternoon, and evening around 8 or 9 pm. I tried to spread out the last feeding so he wouldn't be hungry overnight. Then I learned that even mamas don't necessarily feed them through the night. After that, it was easier to say good night to him, close up the barn, and go inside for the night. Before that, I'd lie awake wondering if he was hungry, and listening for his 'bleating'. In the morning, I'd warm his bottle and head to the barn, which is only one hundred feet or so from my house.

I'd call softly to him as I neared, saying his name, saying good morning, to get him used to my voice and not to startle him. This was to become invaluable following his release, as all I had to do was call his name and he would trot in from wherever he was. There was always something almost magical in those moments of standing in my yard calling him by name and having him come a-runnin'. That same magical feeling would happen time and again with my other fawns.

A word here about the 'bleating' that fawns do. It is much like a lamb or sheep, so much so that when I first heard it I thought someone had snuck one of them into my barn as a joke. Deer are mostly quiet, not routinely vocal, but between mama and her fawn there is definite vocal communication. The mama uses a very deep-pitched, grunting-rumbling sort of sound, conveying a particular message to her fawn, like, 'come over here', 'lie down there', 'mama's on the phone'. The fawn often bleats to call its mama, like, 'I'm hungry', 'I'm hungry NOW', 'I'm here -- where are YOU?' As I was to learn, bleating is also a sign of distress.

The deer experts told me to start him on solid foods such as horse sweet feed in another four to five days. Uh-oh, another thing my horses would have to share. I hesitated to even mention it to them, but as the reader will discover, I talk a lot to my animals. They were still a bit unhappy being blocked out of their stalls, so I hated to hit them with more disgruntling news right away. I would however eventually mention it to them in casual conversation, in between treats of extra-delicious apples. It was sort of a "you know fellas, these-are-extra-special-apples-I-got-just-for-you-and-John-Doe's-eating-your-grain-now-too-and-aren't-these-just-the-BEST-apples-you've-ever-tasted?!" They barely blinked an eye. Aside from horse sweet feed, I was also to start him on carrot and apple pieces, and a mineral type salt lick, another good source of energy. After a week or so of introducing him to solid foods, I was to begin weaning him off the milk. It sounded like another fairly simple plan to me. Things were moving right along without a hitch.

Chapter 3

For the first several days of John Doe's stay, I'd blocked off not only the stall Dutch doors from the run-in shed, but the run-in shed itself. I used a two-by-four at the corner of the end of the barn and ran it across to connect with the fence just outside the run-in shed. This was to let John Doe settle in as smoothly as possible and get used to his new temporary home, with all its sounds, before having to contend with the horses and all their sounds being right outside his door.

The main barn doors are sliders on tracks which squeaked; the stall door hinges groaned; the steamer trunk with the horse feed made a ratchety noise; the horses had their peculiar sounds, snorting, whinnying, hooves reverberating on the ground. One pasture is just below the barn, on the run-in shed side, so even the sounds of the horses pulling the grass as they graze carried into John Doe's stall. He was very alert and his ears would perk up, literally, and wave back and forth like two furry little radar units as he followed the sounds, trying to discern what they meant. He didn't seem particularly startled by any of the noises, although I continually talked to him to help him be at ease. I also began leaving the radio on, with a classical station playing softly. A little Beethoven or Rimsky-Korsakov never hurt anyone.

Soon, introducing him to Elmo and Ebony seemed like a good idea. I have no notes about this but am fairly certain I did this on a day when Sally was here, not knowing what sort of reactions would come from either the horses or John Doe. I stayed in the stall with him, and Sally did the letting-in of the horses. Fortunately it wasn't one of those days when the horses were 'feeling their oats' and ran to get under the run-in shed or into a stall. For two species that use foot stomps as a means of communication, not a stomp was made during both introductions. Each horse calmly walked to the open Dutch door of the stall, and peered in, sniffing.

Ebony was the first to come. Being a Plantation Walkin' Horse, he was a big fellow, but with a particularly massive head that filled much of the open space above the Dutch door. He must have looked extra-huge to John Doe, but it didn't scare him. He ventured fairly close to Ebony and they bobbed heads back and forth and sniffed one another from a safe distance. The head-bobbing and sniffing went on for a short time, and then as I remember, it was Ebony who turned away first. I don't know if something had caught his attention, or if he had just decided 'ok, I've met the little guy - - now I've got some grass grazing to do.'

Then it was Elmo's turn. John Doe stood at attention, ears on alert, looking intently at him, as if he were studying him. I knelt beside John Doe, patting and talking to him, and after some seconds, he walked right over to where Elmo's head was hanging down over the stall door. For several seconds the two stood with their heads inches apart, and for a brief moment I was a little hesitant about what was going to happen. I needn't have been. Just a moment later, each craned their necks forward - - they were touching noses. A lot of mutual sniffing went on. They were definitely interested in each other species-to-species, accepted one another, and seemed to like each other. It was during this first nose-to-nose visit between Elmo and John Doe that I captured the photo on the next page which is one of my prized fawn photos.

I have not yet touched on the topic of his 'potty-training', or to be more succinct, how you teach a fawn "to go", because that's exactly what you have to do. It's what his mama would do in the wild. It is literally hands-on, with a cotton ball dipped in a little warm water. Perhaps you remember the old summer camp trick of sticking your cabin-mate's hand in warm water while he or she slept, and then getting the giggles when they either wet the bed, or made it to the bathroom just in time, all the while yelling that they were going to get you back? It's just about as simple with a fawn, although you don't dip its hoof in the warm water.

You have to actually stimulate it with warm wet cotton balls to get both urinary and bowel movements going. With each, the trick is to move your hand out of the way a millisecond before things get going, not too early or nothing will happen, and not too late, or you'll have to go wash up, again. So the real trick is to know when, precisely, that latter moment is. I learned after only a few what are best described as moist experiences. John Doe was a fast learner so I only had to do this procedure for about three or four days. Then he was going on his own.

Early on, the Vet came with his portable x-ray machine to determine the extent and specifics of John Doe's leg/knee injury. John Doe was an excellent patient. He stood quietly as I held him in this or that position, while the man with the odd-looking machine prodded and poked around, and moved the machine right next to his leg. I was as proud as any mama could be at how well-behaved my little boy was. The Vet called later with the report: it was a hairline fracture, also known as a green-stick fracture, which yes, could be repaired, though the prognosis was uncertain. I'll go more into this later, but we decided the only choice was to do the surgery. He could not have been released into 'the wild' with his bum leg.

For now though, we forged onward and upward. I introduced solid foods slowly as directed, and in small amounts: at first, a handful of the horse sweet feed, and little bites of carrots, apples, and grapes. He took an immediate liking to them all. I began to wean his milk supply which he wasn't crazy about initially. He knew he wasn't getting the same amount and would trot around me frantically looking for another bottle, or a refill, and then he would stop right in front of me and look up with those soulful brown eyes as if to say 'HEY, is this some kind of joke? Where's the rest?!' Once the supplements of solid foods began, and then increased, the weaning became easier and easier. He would dive into the grain and treats with the same gusto previously reserved for his bottles.

I should backtrack here, and try to describe what it's like to feed a bottle to a hungry fawn. For the life of me I don't know how the mamas stay upright -- except they have the advantage of four legs versus my measly two. And they know what to expect. First, the fawn spreads its little legs apart, as if it's preparing for a tug-of-war with a moose. If such an encounter were to ever take place, I've little doubt that the fawn would hold its own at least for a time. Who would guess how mighty these little critters could be? Not I certainly, at least not at first. They look as if they're doing a fawn's version of a split, with those little legs very widely and very firmly planted. Once they're planted, they are Planted. Even with his one bum leg, John Doe managed to gain a firm stance, and I mean a Firm Stance. Once planted, he gave up no ground. The following photo, although it is of a later fawn, best shows 'The Stance'.

Not only is their stance incredibly solid, the force with which they tug and drink is unbelievably strong. I was so unprepared for it that first time that I got pulled off balance and nearly fell over on him. Somehow I managed to fall just to my knees, thrust the bottle-less hand into the sawdust to catch and steady myself, and keep the bottle upright. He never missed a beat. I'm not sure he even noticed I'd fallen.

From then on at least, I knew what to expect and how to brace myself before the assault began. And brace myself I did. [I will explain my counter-measures in a moment.] Considering that I weighed about 80-plus pounds more than he, it's quite something that I had to brace myself at all.

The other amazing thing is how fast they drink. I was never able to actually time it, as I had no hand available to hold a stop watch, nor did I ever manage to plant my bottle-less hand, the one flung against the wall helping to hold me stable and upright, the one with the watch, with the watch dial facing up so I could see the second hand.

I did try to count though, and memory tells me he finished an 8-oz bottle in about 10 seconds, sometimes less. As with nursing babies, you have to take care that at the end of the bottle the little one doesn't suck in air. I kid you not, it took all my might to break his suction hold on the bottle.

My usual strategy became to hide the bottle behind my back as I entered the stall. He knew I had a bottle, and he'd race around me, poking his nose here and there, looking intently for it, sometimes 'climbing' up my legs, or arms if I was dumb enough to leave them dangling, to find it. I learned right away that I had to move quickly. I also learned to wear long-sleeve somewhat bulky shirts and pants at bottle-time. [football padding would have been appropriate] I would put my back against a stall wall, slide down it, [hence the bulky shirt, to minimize the amount of skin being scraped off against the raw wood], drop to my knees, spread them apart as far as they would go, put my left hand and arm out to the side against the wall as an extra bracer, then produce the bottle in my right hand, held high and pointing down so he could get right to drinking. It was sort of like being on the old game show "Beat the Clock". I think my fastest get-ready maneuver was six seconds, but I was always trying to improve on that because the slower I was the more intent he was on getting those lips suctioned to that bottle.

For the most part this method worked pretty well, and when the bottle was finished, we were both still upright. That was definitely a plus from my point of view. A most endearing thing fawns do during feeding, in captivity or in the wild with mama, is a constant wagging and wiggling of their fannies and bobbed white-tipped tails. It's one of those things in nature that makes you smile. Well, it makes me smile.

Our new food regimen went along very smoothly for many days. He would take 4-5 oz of milk, supplemented with grain and treats, four times a day. Little by little I increased the solids and decreased the milk. He was going to the bathroom on his own. He was also drinking water and working on the salt lick. Things were moving along nicely.

Chapter 4

Then things started becoming a little erratic, as at times he seemed not to be very hungry. From my reading, which I've not mentioned but was still doing lots of, and from conversations with the local deer experts and my Vet, it seemed as if this wasn't totally unusual or unexpected. As the fawn grows, and starts on different food stuffs, appetites can vary and fluctuate, as well as output. They told me to continue to monitor everything and keep them posted on any further changes.

With John Doe's appetite fluctuations, his overall intake had slowed considerably, and he was not getting the amounts he needed. The feed times now went through the night, depending on his intake up to night-time. Sally offered to spell me, often coming at 11 pm to go 'on duty'. I would go inside to lie down and hopefully sleep a bit. Then I would relieve her at some point. We each took turns staying in his stall, sometimes just resting, sometimes catching a few winks when he did. This was the beginning of quite a few nights like this, and this period was to get more stressful, iffy and dicey, for John Doe, and for us.

Along with the appetite fluctuations, something else was occurring. He was not going to the bathroom as routinely as before. I thought maybe he'd forgotten that he knew how to do this on his own. So I even began using the cotton balls again, but that didn't work. I'd called my Vet to fill him in on all of this, and he said to keep close track of his elimination, and any straining, and to keep him informed. I had to call him very soon after this phone call, because things took a very bad turn very quickly.

At some point for reasons unknown, but it just sometimes happens with fawns, their digestion lags in development, and elimination gets slowed or blocked. Perhaps it has something to do with orphaned fawns in particular, lacking something they would normally get from mama's milk in the way of protective elements or aids to digestion. But one afternoon, when I found my normally quiet docile little fellow lying down in the stall thrashing about, it was obvious something was terribly wrong.

He was bleating very loudly which was about as heart-wrenching a sound as I've ever heard, and it was the first time I'd ever heard him make any sound. At first I thought it must be his bum leg, but he was hardly moving it. Something seemed to be going on higher up than his leg. He was throwing his head violently, first in one direction then in another, sometimes scraping it against the rough raw poplar of the stall walls. He would throw it back toward his flanks and sort of nip at them.

A light went on in my head. His thrashing, nipping at his flanks, and obvious distress, were very similar to what a horse with colic does. I'd been through it with Ebony. After some touch-and-go moments with him, he had come through fine, which encouraged me as far as John Doe's prognosis. To help protect his head from banging against the stall walls, I mounded sawdust up the walls. Then I raced to phone my Vet and the deer experts.

I described his symptoms and actions, and his bleating. Their immediate and united diagnosis was that his digestive and/or elimination systems were blocked. And he was in pain. They made a game plan. I understood immediately from what they said that we were in a full-blown emergency. I phoned my 'on-call' friend Sally saying "HELP!" Fortunately she was home and available. As soon as she arrived, I was off to the Vet's to pick up the meds that would hopefully relieve his pain and get his systems working again.

One of the meds was Banamine, a non-steroidal anti-inflammatory; one was Tribrisson, an antibiotic; and last was Dipyrone, a muscle relaxant. All were to be given by injection. Hmmm. My Vet gave me directions on how much and often to administer each. Thank Heavens several years earlier he had taught me how to give shots to my horses and dogs. So at least I was fairly comfortable giving shots, to certain animals -- to pets anyway. With horses, you put them in cross-ties; dogs you put on a leash and tell them to 'sit' and 'stay'. Um, scusi Dr. Vet, exactly what method is it you use with a fawn? He explained where the shots were to be given anatomically, the front of the shoulders and backs of the thighs, where it's extra fleshy and where it's "less likely you'll hit anything vital."

That "anything vital" got my attention right quick and I said "aw jeeeez." He reminded me that he'd told me that very same thing when I'd had to give Penicillin shots to Ebony for a period of many days, alternating injection sites, and that I'd done fine. That gave me some momentary reassurance. He also reminded me of the little tip he'd given me -- to give the skin a quick pinch with the fingernail just before poking in the needle. Then he explained that whatever it took to get the shots into the fawn needed to be done, no matter what. I was to give him one shot of each of the three drugs as soon as I got home. Ever an encourager, his last words to me as I headed out his office door were "you can do it -- you'll do fine." That was to become my mantra for the next several days, and I repeated it the whole way home.

I was also to pick up an enema kit for infants, because after giving him the shots and waiting a short period of time, I was to give him an enema. This sent my imagination into overdrive as I tried to envision how *this* would go, on top of giving the shots. No one had ever mentioned that in raising a fawn I might have to give it shots or enemas. Time for another well-thought-out, this time firmer ecclesiastical prayer, "GAWDD, MORE HELP PLEASE!"

I did the round trip to and from my Vet's with a stop at the pharmacy in record time and arrived back home with the meds and supplies. I was to give one shot each, the Banamine, Tribrisson and Dipyrone immediately. That meant three anatomical spots I had to pick out, get to, and be able to use the first go-round. I remember heading to the barn with fear and trepidation, not only wondering how John

Doe was doing, but how I was going to deal with the new protocols we, Sally and I, and thank heavens it *was* 'we', were going to have to be following for an unknown number of hours or days.

John Doe was quiet at the moment, and lying down, so I quickly fixed the first shots while quietly explaining to Sally what 'we' were going to be doing. As I explained the 'routine', my eyes were rolling and hers were getting as big as saucers. [Swell, the ga-ga leading the ga-ga.]

I slowly knelt beside John Doe, talking softly to him while Sally patted him. I decided to go for the back of the thigh on one leg for the first injection, as he was lying on his side with all four legs stretched out making all potential target areas relatively exposed. Of course I first had to swab the area with alcohol. To save time and stress, though I'm not sure for whose sake more, mine or his, I swabbed both back thighs and one shoulder so all sites were ready and I wouldn't have to stop in between shots to swab. He remained calm and quiet while I swabbed. So far so good.

I decided to go for the harder-to-reach spot first, the back leg that was under the front one. I didn't use the quick fingernail pinch first because I didn't want to startle him, following that time-honored adage of 'let sleeping dogs lie'. I nudged the top back leg just a smidge out of the way with my left hand, kept my hand on it, then slid my right hand to the bottom thigh and quickly poked in the needle and plunged. I did aspirate first, quickly, to make sure I'd not hit a vein or artery. He continued to lie still. It was good he was calm, as by now I felt my body temperature in the hundreds of degrees, my heart rate in the thousands, and my blood pressure off the charts. I took a deep breath and gave the injection in the other thigh.

Two down and one to go. He still remained calm, offering no protest or resistance. Only later did I realize this was due to the stress he was in, and that the meds had gotten started just in the nick of time. In other words, we could have lost him. Moving my hands to the shoulder of his top leg, I gave the last injection of the series. I let out a huge sigh of relief, told him what a good boy he was, and leaned over and nuzzled him. I'd taken to doing that a lot, so he was used to it and seemed to like it. He would always nuzzle back, which he did even then despite his pain and stress. It may be that it reminded him of his days with his mama when she would do the same, as whenever I did it he seemed to become sort of transfixed.

The Vet could not pinpoint how long it might be before the drugs took effect, but said to wait a good half hour or so before doing the enema. At first I'd only told Sally about the shots. When the first three had been given, she said "good job-glad we're through for now", which seemed the opportune moment to tell her we weren't quite through and what lay ahead. So I said, "wellllll, not quite...after about a half hour, we have to give him an enema". Now *her* eyes were rolling and *mine* were big as saucers. [Welcome back to ga-ga land.]

John Doe was still lying down, looking a bit woozy, or peaceful. It was hard to tell. More to the point, I wasn't experienced enough to determine exactly which was more accurate, but it was probably a combination of both. He wasn't bleating any more which I took as a good sign, that the meds had kicked in to relieve pain. To prepare for giving the enema, I went to the house to get a thermos of hot water and a bowl, then back to the stall, got the cotton balls and bulb syringe ready, and mixed the fleet enema 'stuff'. It was close to an hour before John Doe began to stir. He got to his feet a bit unsteadily, and as we stabilized him from each side, it seemed like the time to give him the enema. It went incredibly smoothly, although it produced no results. He was however very interested in some milk or food. I checked with the Vet as to what to do, whether to feed him, and if so, what. He suggested trying water first, then just a little milk, but no solids. John Doe lapped at the water for only a few seconds, but was definitely interested in milk, although I gave him just 2 ounces. He was obviously feeling better.

Rather than give a daily blow-by-blow of the shots and enemas, suffice it to say that the next six days were like a roller-coaster. If my notes are accurate, over these six days, we gave him 19 shots and 9 enemas. At times, the drugs seemed to do their thing, the enemas their thing, he would eat a little or drink a little, and go to the bathroom sporadically. So progress would be made, only to backslide within hours or during the next day. I was frequently on the phone with the Vet or deer experts.

We were also having to monitor his temperature, rectally, and at times he had a low-grade fever, or a high one. During the worst of his tummy troubles, his temperature was 102.6 to 103. Normal temperature for a deer is 100 to 102. Anything over 102 or under 100 is trouble. At one point, he also developed a slight case of pneumonia and dehydration which not only compromised his health even more but complicated his recovery, and threatened to sabotage our efforts to get him well. There were times when he definitely did not want a shot or enema, and there were struggles that were difficult not just physically, but emotionally for us as well. I kept reminding us of the Vet saying that we had to get the shots and enemas done no matter what it took. Either Sally or I was with John Doe around the clock for those six days. When it was shot or enema time we were both there.

The hardest part, aside from sometimes having to subdue him to give the shots or enemas, were the times when he would thrash about, throwing his head around wildly, and bleat. Sometimes he would fall down if he weren't already lying down, and sometimes he would hit his head or some other body part against the stall wall. By the end of these episodes it looked like we were running a blanket store on the side, we had so many of them piled up against the stall walls.

Finally!, the breakthrough day came when John Doe was at last out of the woods, with his digestion working, output and intake balanced, no fever or dehydration, going to the bathroom routinely again, and acting like a normal healthy fawn. His appetite returned, and increased, and over just a few days we could see him begin to fill out and grow. Joyous "Hallelujahs!" could be heard coming from my barn! Our hearts were elated to see him back to feeling good. Secondarily was a deep gratitude that we didn't have to give any more shots or enemas.

Chapter 5

Now somewhere in the middle of all this, as hard as it is to believe, the Vet performed surgery on his leg. My notes report the date of his surgery as July 7, and it must have been done when his intake and output were still good. While I do have some fairly specific notes, especially when things went south with his tummy and intestines, and throughout the shots and enemas, there is no mention and I have no recollection of the cast presenting any real problems in doing either.

I also do not have specific notes regarding the surgery or recovery period. If I'd known I'd one day want to write about it, and that there would be other fawns to come, I'd have been a better reporter, maybe, or, I hope. When notes are lacking and I try to recall specific things, sometimes all I get is haze. I do remember taking him to the Vet's for the surgery, waiting, and bringing him home still very groggy. I also remember there was very little we had to do with the cast, other than changing the sock covering it when it got too dirty or damp from spilled water.

As far as the surgery itself, the Vet and deer experts and I discussed the pros and cons, potential prognoses, which ran the gamut of poor to excellent healing and mobility post-op. There was no way to predict what course things would take. But there was simply no way that he could be released with his leg in the condition it was. Yes, he could get around in the stall, even fairly steadily, and after we put up the little fenced-in enclosure just outside the barn's front double door, he could walk around in a larger space. He would sometimes even trot a bit, or do the little play-jumps I mentioned before that are an invitation to play. But released 'into the wild', he'd need stamina and speed, and that fourth leg for push-offs and balance. With the fracture, he would be severely handicapped. So a joint decision was made that there was no choice but surgery.

In conversations with the Vet and deer experts after his bowel problems were resolved, there were mixed reviews as to whether the anesthetic contributed to these problems. But surgery presented one of those catch-22 situations that just had to be done. I'd been doing lots of praying for John Doe, about his tummy troubles, then for the surgery and a good outcome. Those prayers were enjoined by ones from Sally, the Vet, and a whole group of folks at my church. We kept them going non-stop. In keeping with his nature, he was very accepting of the cast, which was on for three weeks. He had always enjoyed snuggling and cuddling, and the cast didn't prevent him from continuing to do so.

That's co-surrogate mama Sally with him in the previous photo. For some reason it wasn't until the day of his release that I thought to have her take some photos of me with John Doe. Oh well, one can't think of everything.

By the way, when I talk about him, or later fawns, being released into 'the wild', what I mean is the small neighborhood in which I live. It is on top of a hill, in the country, surrounded by woods, fairly far from any roads, with several creeks, ponds and lakes on adjacent properties. Our hilltop neighborhood and adjacent properties encompass about 600 acres, most of which don't allow hunting, except for one property owner, so except for the occasional poacher it is a very safe environment in which to release fawns.

July 31 was the day the cast was removed, and I remember it as though it was yesterday, no haze here. The Vet had warned me not to expect too much, and to be prepared that John Doe might not be able to bend that knee, ever. That was a scary thought, as it meant he would be at a definite disadvantage in the wild escaping predators. Deer's legs, the strength and flexibility of them, are their tickets to freedom, escape, and safety, invaluable in covering and leaping great distances that give them the edge over predators.

That day of the cast removal, I waited in the barn with Sally for the Vet. We prayed that all would be healed and that his knee would bend. He'd cleared the hurdles of his tummy and digestion problems, slight pneumonia and dehydration. Now there was just his leg. The Vet arrived, and he prayed with us for John Doe, that the surgery was not only successful but that his knee would bend. John Doe must have been the most prayed-for fawn ever.

The Vet removed the cloth bandaging from around the cast. Then he took off the cast. John Doe was as good a patient during the cast removal as when the x-rays had been taken, standing quietly as the mini buzz saw cut through it. We three waited to see what he might do, if anything, not knowing how he'd react. Once it was off, he stood there staring at us, probably wondering why we three were sitting there staring at him. No longer able to stand the suspense, the

Vet gently took John Doe's leg in his hands, and slowly attempted to bend it at the knee. And GLORY BE, HALLELUJAH! RAISE THE FLAG! IT BENT! I think we all had tears in our eyes. We cheered the Vet, and we cheered John Doe. It was a *grand* celebration. Photo below was taken the day after cast was removed, clearly showing his now-bendable leg!

Now this next part I do not remember as I sit here today 18 years later, but it's in my notes which do trigger another hazy recollection. My note says "cast off!-knee bends! -- John Doe jumped over the stall door!" He'd leapt over the door that leads to the run-in shed. Fortunately the horses had been blocked out of the run-in shed so at least he didn't crash into one of them. The Dutch door is four feet high, and he cleared it, sailing out of sight. I'm sure I screamed in shock, and don't remember what anyone else did, but I undid the latch and bolted out the door. He was standing just on the other side looking at me, and I think he was as surprised as we were at what he'd done. Thank Heavens he didn't keep running.

I started talking quietly to him, first telling him he'd scared the bejeebees out of us and *what* was he thinking!, then saying we needed to go back into the stall. I began to coax and steer him along, and back into the stall he went without a problem. Phew!-disaster averted. It was that day that I blocked every opening of the stall with strong netting, stretched taut and nailed securely. Once the netting was up I knew he wouldn't be making any future great escape leaps over stall doors.

As soon as he was back in the stall, the Vet rechecked his leg and thankfully, all was fine. He said since John Doe could obviously leap tall stall doors in a single bound, it was an excellent sign that his leg was virtually as good as new, perhaps even stronger than the others. Another "Phew" and sighs from us all. Except for John Doe whose only 'comment', as he started nuzzling each of us, was 'ok, bring on some milk and food'.

Chapter 6

It was back to normal, and more than just normal as we'd known it up to then. Normal was really normal as now we had a fawn who was tip-top healthy, with *all four* legs in good working order. Considering all he'd been through, and how touch-and-go it had been at times, John Doe was one staunch little trooper through it all.

I made no notes about this, but it's standing out to me now. Not once throughout the ordeals he endured, his bad leg, the blockage of his intestines and the pain that brought, all those shots and enemas, did he lash out at me, or Sally. Not once did he act mean or try to kick or bite us. That is rather remarkable to my way of thinking. I've had pets I raised, dogs and horses, who in their pain or distress tried to nip or kick me. I know it wasn't that they wanted to hurt me, they just sometimes reacted instinctively. John Doe never did that.

Despite becoming somewhat domesticated while living with me and in my barn, he was still a wild animal at heart and by nature, so it would seem much more natural to expect it to be the wild animal, not the pet dog or horse, who would lash out. Although none of the other fawns I raised had problems like John Doe, several did require some meds or a shot or two, and their demeanor was the same as John Doe's -- quiet, accepting, always gentle and meek. So to say that there is something especially soft and kind about the heart and soul of fawns and deer is, I believe, true.

Feedings were back on schedule, his appetite was excellent, he was going to the bathroom regularly, and he was becoming more playful and interested in the outside world. I removed the two-by-four that had blocked off the run-in shed. The horses could then come under it and visit with John Doe through the netting, which they frequently did. I also opened the other stall to them, and the three became very accustomed to one another's presence. There were lots of days when the horses would lie under the run-in shed, which would put them just outside John Doe's stall. He could hear them breathing softly and would go over to the door and just stand there with his ears waving as he listened.

Some days, I would close all the barn doors to the outside, open the stall doors to the inside of the barn, and let him walk around the entire barn. I made sure to move any potentially dangerous items, like pitch forks. It seemed a good idea to expand his world, besides he needed to begin to stretch and build up his legs and muscles. He had a good time investigating every nook and cranny he could get to, poking and sniffing in all the corners, and especially the bales of hay. I took to taking a good book and cup of tea to the barn for these outings, and I'd sit on the lower bales of hay while he milled about the barn.

At some point prior to his cast removal, we constructed a fenced-in area outside the front doors of the barn so we could let him out for fresh air, sunlight and grass. It was just a wire mesh fence, though fairly sturdy. He could easily have jumped it but seemed content to peer through it, nibble at grass, or lie down and enjoy the warmth of the sun. I hung strips of white cloth on it to delineate its boundaries for him. It was also a good opportunity for him to begin to see other deer as they strolled through the pastures, and he perked up at the sight of them and would watch them closely. Interestingly enough, they never seemed to notice him, or us with him. Or if they did, they weren't curious enough to wander over for a closer look. I think he really enjoyed these outings.

As I remember it was a rather dry summer so he was able to have frequent outings in his pen. Though at some point he would have to experience bad weather, now that his release seemed assured, I hoped that by that time he'd have been on his own long enough, and gained enough self-confidence and self-sufficiency not to be afraid. And I hoped from his travels that he would also have gained a good working knowledge of the area and surrounding woods to find protection from the elements. I also hoped he would know my barn would always be a safe haven for him.

The second week of August a good friend of my Mother's who had heard I was raising a fawn called to see about bringing some of her grand-children for a visit. Late morning on August 12 she arrived with her two daughters and their five young children, ages four to eight or so. I gave them a brief history of how John Doe came to be living in my barn, what he was like, what he liked to eat, how old he was, and that sort of thing. I told them we all had to talk softly and move slowly, told them his name and that they could say it to him quietly when they met him. I went ahead to get in the stall with him to tell him he had company. The little troop came in, went straight to the bales of hay, and sat down without so much as a whisper, just as they'd been asked to do.

I opened the stall door, and walked over to them with John Doe coming right by my side. I sat down next to them, and he meandered over to each child, and adult, sniffing them, their shoes, arms and legs, their shorts. None of the kids moved at all, and a few of them murmured "ahhhhh". I could hear little quiet giggles as he touched their skin with his nose, and they were enthralled, with ear-to-ear grins. None of them had ever been this close to a fawn. I gave everyone pieces of apples or carrots to give him.

You'd have thought John Doe had been entertaining groups of visitors forever. He didn't leave out anyone, but 'worked the barn' like a pro, and proceeded to go down the row and gently take each child's offering of apple or carrot. Of course this thrilled each child even more, and they were saying in quiet excitement, "he TOOK if from me!", "he LICKED my fingers!", and things like that. It was wonderful to watch their faces, and to watch his gentle approach and interactions with them. They stayed for about an hour, and John Doe received several Thank You notes from them later.

John Doe's next 'show' was August 25. A friend of Sally and her husband's, and mine, who'd grown up here, was visiting and wanted to meet John Doe. He was as enchanted with him as the kids had been. Below, friend Fuz meets furry fawn.

He wrote me a note when he'd returned home: "I think all the time about the wonderful time I had with John Doe in your barn. What a beautiful, delicate gift you were given. It just amazes me that I actually played with a wild animal!"

Chapter 7

Summer days were speeding by quickly. I'd begun to realize that my time with John Doe, at least with him living in my barn and me playing his mama and having these incredible one-on-one experiences with a fawn, would be coming to a close. The deer experts had advised me that once he was well, eating solids only and regularly, I should release him, and well before Fall. And here we were already at the end of August.

I don't remember who suggested 'tagging' him, but it seemed a good idea, making it easy for me to spot him, but more, it would hopefully deter any poaching hunters from targeting him. It was bright yellow so it would stand out, and I wrote his name on it. I also got an extra in case the first got dislodged in his travels.

August 30 the Vet came and placed the tag in his left ear. It was much like piercing one's ear. The procedure didn't bother John Doe at all. Once again, true to form, he was as good as gold while the Vet inserted the clip that held the tag in place. He didn't show any signs that it bothered him.

The Vet left and Sally came over later. We let him out into the fenced-in enclosure and as I remember spent most of the afternoon in the pen with him. He had his food at the regular times, and at some point, we decided this would be a good day for his release. It was a bright sunny day, not too hot or humid. He'd been watching several groups of deer who had been hanging out in the back field, and his ID tag was in place.

John Doe seemed more interested in the fields beyond his enclosure and the barn this day than he had shown before, and this seemed a good sign, that he was ready to meet the world. Knowing that he was not only physically well now, but also mentally ready for the world outside the one he'd known in my barn for the last two months, helped me accept his leaving and encouraged me about how he would fare on his own.

Sally's husband came over late afternoon, and brought pizza for dinner. The exact sequence of events isn't clear to me now, nor did I take notes about it. But basically, John Doe sort of released himself, which all in all, made it a bit easier on me.

He'd gone back into his stall. Sally's husband helped us open up the fenced enclosure at the barn entrance. Sally and I went into the stall with John Doe. I opened the Dutch door to the run-in shed. He sort of peered out, craning his neck to see along the sides of the barn. Ebony came and stood outside the stall. Thank Heavens he didn't decide to come *in* the stall. With Sally sitting on the stoop and John Doe standing there it could have been disastrous.

He wasn't in any rush to step out of the stall, but rather seemed content to just look out the door. He didn't venture out of the stall into the barn either, where he would have seen that the fence was gone. It seemed he might take some coaxing, though we weren't sure exactly how to go about that. We decided to leave the stall and barn, and figure out how we would get him to do the same. While we were discussing it, after a last look at the security of his stall, John Doe released himself.

He didn't go far at all, just behind the barn. And finally! a photo of me with him.

I had thought ahead and put some of his treats in my pocket. I may have thought this might keep him around a bit longer, as I didn't know if once freedom was attained, he'd be gone for good. But I also wanted him to know that even free, he could always get treats from me.

Little by little he began to venture farther away from my barn. Early on I learned just how responsive he was to his name. I would call him, and he'd stop and look toward me, and then either come to me or wait until I got to him. I was probably very much like those annoying clingy mothers who just won't hand over their child on the first day of kindergarten, but prolong the goodbye which doesn't help anyone, mother or child. But he finally began running around the fields, and what was so exciting and heartwarming was to see him prance around and make huge leaps using his once-broken leg. On top of that, to see him so healthy and fit after all he'd been through was absolutely wonderful!

He explored the wooded areas surrounding the barn and house, and began nibbling on vegetation, just as he was supposed to do as a now 'wild' deer. Watching him made my heart smile, and made me once again feel so grateful for all the help from the Vet, deer experts, and Sally in his raising. It was truly a group effort.

For the rest of the afternoon and into the early evening Sally and I, [her husband stayed at my house], traveled along with John Doe as he roamed. He did a lot of investigating, sniffing here and tasting there. He seemed to know instinctively that part of his routine needed to be to browse and feed on different vegetations, and he seemed to be liking what he was tasting. A few times he disappeared from view. All I had to do was call him and there he'd be, which just made me giggle. Never could I have imagined that one day I would be in the woods near my home, calling a fawn by his name and he'd come in response. I've had dogs who weren't nearly as responsive and who'd been through Obedience Training!

After about two hours, John Doe wandered off into the woods again, and we took that opportunity to head back to my house. He didn't follow, nor did he come to the barn or house looking for us again that evening. That was a good sign, as far as his independence and self-confidence. Though I must admit it was a bittersweet time for me. I was going to miss him living in my barn and the special relationship we had.

Deep down though, I was excited for him that at last, after all his troubles, he was free and able to be a real deer. While he didn't come in again that evening, we did catch glimpses of him leaping through my back field, or trotting and prancing around in it, or heading off into the woods, as we munched on pizza courtesy of Sally's very patient husband. We also drank a toast to John Doe.

Since I'll be using the term 'in', as in 'come in', often, what I mean is coming to and being around my property, house or barn. At dark, Sally and her husband left, and I went to the barn to spend a little time with the horses, give them some hay, and freshen up the stall bedding. No bad weather was in sight so I did block them out of the run-in shed, and thereby the stalls, and left the barn lights on, just in case John Doe came back sometime during the night needing a dose of the security of his stall. Then I 'closed up shop' and headed to bed after a long soak in a hot bath. Truth be told, I couldn't wait to get to sleep so morning would come and I could get outside to see if John Doe was around. Several times through the night I did wake up wondering where he was, and what and how he was doing.

The next morning I awoke around 5 am, in optimistic anticipation and excitement that John Doe would be here. I fixed a bowl of grain and treats, and headed out to the barn to give the horses their breakfast. The first face I saw, in the field just behind the barn, was John Doe! I was elated! The minute he saw me he came running. It was a grand reunion for me even though it had been only about ten hours since I'd seen him. I was so glad to see that he had made it through his first night alone and on his own, and was doing well. He seemed glad to see me, as a friend I know, but because I had his grain and treats.

As I held out his bowl for him, I could practically hear Elmo and Ebony sighing 'aw no, here we go again with the fawn feeding.' He was hungry, but not in a 'hurry-up-I'm-starved' fashion. That was good as it meant he had been finding food. He ate calmly, unhurriedly, as was his usual way. He was very relaxed and that was a good sign. I had no idea if he'd yet met any other deer, but I hoped so. He was so easy-going that I felt he would be accepted by them. From that morning on, I did keep a running record of when and where I saw and/or was with him, at least for a time.

Chapter 8

My Fall was spent mostly with him. It was reminiscent of my days with Little Lone Fawn, only John Doe was obviously much tamer, and knew me much better. After all, he had lived with me, in my barn, and he and I had spent so much time together in general, but also many a night together when he was ailing. Ours had been a real hands-on relationship from the get-go. I'd bottle-fed him, and he had had to rely on me for his food and care. So there was definitely a bond between us that hadn't existed with Lone Fawn.

A neighbor couple, Mary and Dick, who had become great friends since I built my home up here, had also come over to meet John Doe prior to his release. Their house and land was at the other end of our little hilltop neighborhood, and it abutted the largest expanse of woods, the property I mentioned where the owner did allow hunters. They are big animal folks, with dogs, chickens, and a pony for their grand-daughter when she came to live with them.

As an example of just how animal-minded they are: I got a ride down our hill with Mary one winter day. As we drove along, I thought I was going a bit wacky because I kept hearing, or thought I was hearing, a sort of 'clucking' inside her car. Finally I said so to her, and she burst out laughing as out from under her sweatshirt she produced a rooster! His name escapes me at the moment, although 'Chip' rings a dim bell, but he was obviously a card-carrying member of their family who enjoyed car rides and snuggling in Mary's sweatshirt!

Kind and generous souls that they are, Mary and Dick bought two nifty free-standing wood self-feeders for wildlife -- the kind where you put food in the top and as the animal eats, more automatically slides down into the feeding trough at the bottom. They put one below their house, on their lawn just at the edge of the woods. The other, they gave to me and I put it near my barn. He would come to know both these feeding stations very well, and could be found at one or the other at some point almost every day. He still wanted his treats though, despite foraging for his own food and despite these two feeding stations.

All through September he hung around and traveled to and from the same places, at least as far as I could tell. His main areas were: my back field, or the pasture below the barn where he would often browse at the same time the horses grazed; the pastures and fields just outside and around my barn; the barn itself, and he did venture inside it several times for a look around, never staying long. I often wondered if it brought back memories to him, and if so, I hoped they were the good ones that came to the forefront.

Other main areas were the yards around my house, the woods between my house and barn and one neighbor's house, and the beginning of the woods near Mary and Dick's, the property where the hunters were allowed. The first time I found him fairly far onto that property gave me great pause, so much so that I hurriedly ushered him back to Mary and Dick's, the feeding station and safety. He was cooperative and came along with me, but just as I did that, I realized I could not be with him every minute and could not always protect him. I had to accept that there would be times that he would venture onto that property, and potentially come into harm's way when hunting season began.

The bigger picture was that there are many other potential dangers, aside from hunters, that can jeopardize young fawns' health and survival their first year, and I had to accept that I couldn't protect him from those either. I just kept praying lots for him, all the time. Predators like dogs, bear and coyote, parasites, disease, and cars were just a few of the threats. Then there were accidents in the woods, resulting in injuries like broken bones making survival iffy or impossible, or resulting in instant death. Of all these, the only one I could try to have any positive effect on was protecting him from hunters.

It was then that I contacted the owner of the property who allowed hunters, to tell her about John Doe. She put me in touch with the three hunters whom I called to tell them about the fawn with the bright yellow tag in his ear. All three enjoyed hearing about him, were very understanding about my request to please not harm him, and assured me they would be careful and watch out for him.

They also said that responsible, ethical hunters would not target a fawn or yearling, which gave me great hope and encouragement. I also contacted several neighbors on an adjacent hill to spread the word. There is virtually no hunting allowed there, but as they said, poachers had sneaked in over the years. They too promised to keep an eye out for him, and any poachers.

Then Sally and I came up with the idea of posting "No Hunting" signs everywhere we could. We got permission from property owners and decided we would do this not only on foot but on horseback as well. We also decided that we would 'patrol' the woods on horseback during hunting season. I can hear you now, "what were you, *Crazy*?!" In our defense, being almost twenty years ago, people weren't as 'gun-crazy' then; you didn't hear about drive-by shootings and the like. They were kinder, gentler times. Although admittedly we were naïve about the potential danger to us and our horses, we were committed to doing this. I will talk more about our mounted patrol later. For now, back to John Doe's travels and life that Fall.

Chapter 9

As per my notes, practically every day John Doe was here or at Mary and Dick's. Deer establish their territory which usually encompasses three or so miles, and that's where they spend their time -- feeding, resting, bedding, mating, and raising their fawns. Once established, they pretty much remain within their territory. So it seemed John Doe had established his territory.

When I walked along with him, it was much like going for a walk with one of my dogs. He would stop to 'smell the roses' and lots of other scents that were enticing or interesting to him. Sometimes he would lie down for a rest and I'd sit or lie down next to him, talking and patting him. Even though he was now technically wild he still seemed to enjoy the closeness and patting, and though he was obviously thriving on his own, he never turned down a hand with some treats.

He had also begun to chew his cud. Deer are like cows in this respect, though I think they have fewer than the four stomachs cows have. Being ruminants though makes their systems more delicate, and perhaps more susceptible to digestive problems and blockages like those John Doe had experienced. I never discussed it with the Vet or deer experts, but I'm wondering now if perhaps with no example of mama chewing her cud, he didn't know to do that early on, and that contributed to his problems. But then again, maybe young fawns don't chew their cud. The first time I saw him do it was one of these September days when he was about four months old.

Sometime early September, Sally was babysitting her six-month old grand-son Ryan for the day and thought it would be fun to bring him over and see if we could find John Doe and have the two 'babies' meet. John Doe had never met a human baby, so it would be interesting to see what he thought. It was early afternoon when they arrived. We went to Mary and Dick's when John Doe didn't appear at my house. After banging on the feeder just once, John Doe appeared.

Sally held Ryan in her arms at first, to be on the safe side. We greeted and patted John Doe, and as we did, he craned his neck and head up to Ryan's little body, sniffed him all over, and was pretty non-plussed. He then began browsing. Sally felt it was safe to put Ryan down on the grass, though she stayed right beside him. Ryan began picking at the grass, and little by little John Doe worked his way near to where Ryan was half-sitting, half-lounging, and the two little ones 'grazed' side by side.

Ryan did reach out and pat John Doe when he got close enough. He didn't stop grazing, and certainly wasn't bothered by it. He did come to both me and Sally for some patting and nuzzling. He still liked that and of course we both ate it up. They stayed about an hour, and it was a fun peaceful unique sort of visit - - our version of 'two babes in the woods'.

There were many mornings when John Doe was waiting for me and breakfast either just off my deck or just outside the barn. That always started my day off with an extra good feeling and a big grin. He always ate every morsel in his bowl. As the days passed I could tell he was picking up weight, bulk and body fat, which as I've mentioned is critical for a fawn's survival its first winter.

September 26 I found him lying in Mary and Dick's yard, obviously not feeling well. I knew the minute he didn't get up to greet me that something wasn't right.

He was not interested in his bowl of treats, and his eyes had that dull glazed look. Another race to call my Vet, another quick trip to pick up some oral antibiotics, and we were in nursing mode again. He was still in their yard when I returned with a bowl of grapes rolling around in the pink cherry-flavored antibiotic.

Thank God he liked the flavor and gobbled it all because he was to get this every 12 hours for the next several days. I got all the doses into him. After five days of the meds, he was back to normal, on his feed again, eyes clear and bright, and obviously feeling good again. So another hurdle was overcome, and I hoped that was the last one he would have to face.

We had already done some posting, mostly the areas that were his main stomping grounds. September 30 he was in the woods just beyond Mary and Dick's. When I found him this day, standing where he was, it was a photo I couldn't pass up for its pointed and poignant message. I remember at the time hoping it would not turn out to be prophetic in any negative sense. For some reason that I don't recall now, this was the last photo I took of him. His spots had already begun to fade. In another two weeks they disappeared entirely.

Bow hunting season began October 14. Buck with gun began November 20 and went through December 2. Doe and antler-less with gun began December 8 and went through December 31. No hunting was allowed on Sundays, which was a short but welcome respite from worrying about John Doe for at least one day a week. Our posting project had begun around the middle of September. Again, thankfully, Sally joined me in this venture. We spent many hours over many days posting hundreds of acres. We each had those orange hunter vests and hats from riding in previous years during hunting season and we wore them when we posted signs. No wallflowers were we as we posted either; we talked, whistled, sang, prayed, yelled "hello" and "we're NOT deer", loudly.

We did a lot of posting on foot, but at some point we enlisted the aid of the horses. As the crow flies, and with the many horse and deer trails, it was an easy 10-minute trip on horseback from either of our homes to the other's. We would fill backpacks with signs, hammers and nails, saddle up, meet at a designated spot, and start posting. The horses were very patient and well-behaved, and an additional help in being able to post signs from atop them, higher than a human could reach to tear down a sign.

Amazingly we never ran into one hunter. Considering that we posted well into hunting season, it's more amazing that we or our horses weren't shot, or shot at, either with bow or gun. We did always pray before we headed out, and while we were out prayed for protection. We posted until late November. That was when we began patrolling on horseback. We were committed and we were on a mission.

Chapter 10

The weather had turned cold earlier than usual for our area. We had already had some snow, which was definitely early for us. In our county, and perhaps it's true throughout the country, Thanksgiving Day has the largest number of hunters on the prowl. So we met on horseback that morning. It was cold and snow was falling. We patrolled three or four hours. I should explain that we both loved horses and riding, so while patrolling was our objective, getting to ride our horses was a side perk. By mid-afternoon we were really cold and hungry, the snow fall had increased, and the horses could use some warmth and sustenance themselves.

We were near Sally's house, so we stalled the horses in her barn with fresh water and hay, and went inside to join her family for some Thanksgiving fun and fare. There were some out-of-town relatives who were visiting for the holiday, who could not believe we were out doing what we were out doing, even on a good-weather day, let alone this cold snowy one. As I remember, the overall consensus expressed was "y'all are NUTS!" It was late afternoon when we finished having some good food, warm drink and camaraderie. Since there wasn't much daylight left for more patrolling, I rode back to my house alone which was fine, though I'm sure I whistled and sang louder being the lone patroller. My trip home was uneventful.

Backtracking here a bit, as far as John Doe's travels and my times with him, October and November were pretty much repeats of September. He was in a lot during both months.

October 19 he came into the barn with me. Elmo and Ebony were sharing the far stall, both munching on hay, and as John Doe went to say 'hi' to each, the horses gave nickers of greeting. Nice thought, but in 'horse-speak', they may have been saying 'oh no, *him* again'. While I did some mucking out of the stall where Elmo and Ebony were, John Doe milled about, pulling at some hay, and then went back in his stall. As I'd always done, I talked lots to him whenever he was around.

December followed suit in much the same way, except that many days it would be mid or late afternoon before John Doe would appear. There was a reason for this. Deer metabolism begins to slow down in the Fall, preparing for Winter, cold and snow, when they will be less active, which helps preserve their energy and fat reserves which they will need in the harsher weather when vegetation is scarce or non-existent. Once I understood that, from my books and the deer experts, my mind was much more at ease on those days when he would not be in until later. There were still many anxious times of concern about the hunters, and potential poachers, but I had to let go and put him in God's hands to a large degree. When I did, I was able to cope better.

And John Doe continued to come when I called. If he didn't appear right away, I'd call very loudly and at most it was never more than three or four minutes before he'd appear. Some days during hunting season I called him in a lot just to bring him to me and safety. I suppose that wasn't really leaving him in God's hands, but I hoped God understood.

It was disconcerting on days when he wouldn't appear at dawn or soon after, or until dusk. As hunting season draws to a close, I'd heard that hunters who hadn't 'bagged' anything become desperate and agitated, shoot at anything, and cheat on hunting hours, starting earlier and ending later than the stated laws allow. Late December it was often just before dawn or just after dusk especially that I heard guns going off. And of course those are the two most popular travel times for deer, which hunters know and look to take advantage of. When I heard the hunters cheating, I wanted to scream at them, but didn't as I thought I might startle a deer and send it bolting right into the path of one of the guns.

So those last days of December were particularly hard for me. That was to be true with the fawns I later raised. For about 16 years, hunting seasons in general and Decembers in particular, were especially trying. I didn't raise a fawn each of those years, but each one raised would be out there during one or more hunting seasons. Even during the two hiatuses when I didn't raise a fawn, from 1989 to 1994 and 1994 to 1998, the ones I had raised were out there, along with the 'regulars', especially the big bucks with their prized antlers. As you'll read later, at times fawns overlapped, where one I'd raised and released, was still coming in daily for food and treats, and the 'new kid on the block' had just been released. So there'd be two out there in hunting season. To this day hunting seasons are hard for me. I hate the silence of bow season, I hate the noise of gun season, I pray for a lot of misses, and most of all I pray a lot for my 'regulars.'

That Christmas, Mary and Dick gave me a wonderful homemade, hand-made gift. It is a pastoral scene on a wooden base, but not just any pastoral scene. On one side of the base is a figure of a little fawn, standing beside a true-to-detail miniature version of the feeder complete with pieces of grain in the trough. There is a pine tree next to the feeder, and little piles of 'snow' [cotton]. On the other side of the base is a candle ring with holly embedded in it, and inside it is a small glass vase with a votive candle inside it. Other than the deer figure and the glass vase, they made every part of it. It was a very special and obviously meaningful gift. To this day it takes a center spot among my Christmas decorations. The outer candle ring is misshapen from years of hot winter sun coming through the window onto it. [heads-up ye doubters of global warming.]

John Doe was in every day that December, at my place or at Mary and Dick's. December 31, the last day of hunting season, finally came. Oddly, he was in very early that morning. He was back late morning, again mid-afternoon, and then late afternoon. It was reassuring to have him keep coming in so often as I counted down the hours until hunting season's end at 5 pm. It meant that he was sticking close. I had a strong sense that God's hand was very much at work, not only in keeping John Doe close by and safe, but in bringing him in so often which in turn had been keeping me peaceful and sane. I made sure to give Him Extra Thanks that day.

5 pm came and as John Doe came in, I shouted a big "Hallelujah!" It was dusk and from the adjacent hills sporadic gunfire could be heard for another 10 minutes or so. I quickly filled his bowl with grain and treats, and as it was beginning to snow, I hoped he would follow me into the barn. He did. The horses were in their stalls, dry, toasty warm, and having some hay. John Doe was enjoying his treats. The timer for the lighted star above the barn doors clicked on. The guns had stopped. Hunting season was over. Peace and joy. And a brand new year was just around the corner.

Chapter 11

Then it was "Happy New Year!" In the spirit of the holiday, John Doe came galloping in at daybreak January 1, 1990. Fortunately I was up and ready for him. About three more inches of snow had fallen overnight which made him step higher than normal, and it was funny to watch. It was like someone in summer dabbling their toes in the swimming pool's cold water trying to get used to the temperature before taking the plunge. He looked too like a high-steppin' dressage horse, elegant and graceful. I kidded him that I should have named him 'Prancer'. I don't think he got it. This was the most snowfall we'd had yet, so to John Doe this fluffy cold white stuff, now high on his hooves, was a totally new experience.

It didn't take much convincing for him to follow me into the barn with the warm sawdust floor. On most of the days when we had inches of snow on the ground, he readily came into the barn for his food. I had also started a habit of banging on the feeder near my barn and simultaneously calling him. [Does the name Pavlov ring a bell…?] If he was near, he'd come quickly. If he didn't, I'd run up to Mary and Dick's and repeat the banging. He almost always appeared at one or the other feeder by doing this.

In January his patterns slowly started to return to what they'd been in the Fall. With daylight hours increasing little by little each day, the deer's metabolism does the same thing. It begins to pick up and they start to become more active and energetic, though this does not reach its peak until shortly before Spring. But John Doe did start coming in more routinely throughout the days, and starting earlier in the mornings. This was an ongoing process however, and didn't occur overnight, but was spread out over a period of the next two months of Winter.

All through January he was in two or three times a day. Some days he didn't quite finish his bowl, but it was obvious he was thriving and maintaining a good weight.

February 5 he came in, in the company of a mama, a little fawn, and a 'button buck', which is a male fawn who has just the small nubbins of the beginning of his antler growth -- hence the term 'button'. He was with them throughout the month, which warmed my heart no end to know he did have deer friends now, a sort of family. It brought Little Lone Fawn to mind, and when she had finally become part of a family. Like her, John Doe too walked both worlds, mine and the deer's, and had a place in both.

Of course, and I've not yet addressed the issue, and won't in great detail as it is just one more double-edged sword of hand-raising a fawn, but hand-raising inherently creates a bond and comfortableness with humans. There are drawbacks in that they may end up trusting all humans, including ones with guns. It's an almost impossibly fine line to walk, being a surrogate mama raising them long enough to give them their healthiest and strongest start possible in life, letting them go and giving them their wings so to speak, but monitoring them enough to bolster them as needed once freed, and yet have them not get too used to or trusting of humans-at-large.

I shall have to backtrack again. What I need to relate is that John Doe did have one more hurdle to clear. Unlike the previous ones though, this one was discussed and planned for ahead of time, following the advice of the deer experts and my Vet. The issue was about neutering him. The local deer experts put me in touch with the head of the deer research program at Penn State University, a renowned expert in the field. I had several conversations with him, and I do have extensive notes on the information he provided, which was everything from the necessity of neutering a hand-raised buck, to very specific details about what tranquilizers and/or sedatives, and what anesthetics should be used, as well as dosages according to his weight.

He began by saying that with a hand-raised buck, it must be either captivity or castration. Captivity was not an option for John Doe. I'd already been turned down by our local Zoo and its deer pen, and there were no other facilities anywhere nearby. Then he gave two very good reasons and once I heard them I hardly needed further persuasion.

First: neutering at about six to eight months age would pretty much stop regular antler development, making him less of a 'prize', or better, no prize at all to hunters. This was wonderful news to me and reason enough right there to neuter him. Second: it would stem aggressiveness toward whomever had hand-raised him. Say, What? Since I was the one who'd hand-raised him, [or the main one whose property was now his stomping ground], this caught my attention, and neutering sounded like an even better plan. He explained a lot about this aggressiveness -- how extremely dangerous it is to hand-raise a male fawn and then release him un-neutered, or un-neutered for any length of time. At this point in his explanations, this fellow had a captive audience in me.

He went on to explain that 1 lb of muscle fiber per deer, equals 500 per human. Translation? In a fight between a deer and a human, bet on the deer. Once neutered however, "his killing desire toward whomever hand-raised him would be gone." His WHAT! toward WHOM?! Keep in mind, that by the time of my first conversation with this fellow, which was some time in late October or early November, John Doe had already been released, and he and I had been spending many a day together, often lying down right next to one another in the woods. All of a sudden some renowned expert at a big deer research center at a big university is telling me that this sweet little fawn might attack me and try to kill me?!, and that based on that muscle fiber thing, he'd probably succeed? Well, not right away apparently. Gee, that was good news.

He clarified this, that it's not until two to three years of age that this aggressiveness would appear; "when mature, they will hunt you down." The "you" being the one who hand-raised it -- yours truly. Swell. He added that every year, someone who had raised a fawn two to three years earlier and not neutered him, was attacked and killed by that now very grown, very big, very strong, very aggressive buck. Bring on the neutering, I was a full-blown believer. Truth be told, this guy had me back at "stem aggressiveness toward whomever hand-raised him."

Minutes after we hung up I was on the phone with my Vet, passing on all that this deer expert had said, and making plans for his neutering. I think it was that very day that I went to the Vet's and got the drugs I would need to sedate him. As John Doe was only about four months old at this point, neutering him would have to wait until January or February, not the ideal time weather-wise for such an undertaking, but it was what it was.

The deer expert also gave me scads of information and helpful tips on what my jobs would be and how best to do them, before, during and after the Vet did the actual neutering. With the fawn already released, it complicated things a little, and made other things impossible, like withholding food and water for 12 hours prior to the surgery. If he were back in his stall this could have been done, but having been free for many months he wouldn't tolerate being cooped up again, and could get seriously hurt trying to escape. We'd been there, done that, thank you.

This project was going to take ingenuity, flexibility, spontaneity, coordinating, scheduling, timing, and adjusting, and with three different variables -- John Doe, me, and the Vet. Of those three, only two of us could discuss this and work on how best to accommodate things. That meant one wild card in the deck which could be unpredictable. So, our project would definitely include a lot of luck, and a lot of prayer. It would also include some help from Mary and Dick, who were always more than willing to help in any situation but we're particularly so in this one. They'd gotten to know John Doe and wanted to do whatever they could to help him.

And per Murphy's Laws, it would be smart to be ready for the unexpected. We mentally planned to do this the first fairly nice day the first week of February; in other words, one when there wasn't snow on the ground, or predicted, and when it wasn't snowing, or particularly cold or windy. Or, in other words, we were looking for a balmy February day. Back then, almost twenty years ago, we didn't get such days in February. We might just as well plan a reception for visitors from outer space.

Chapter 12

But undaunted, we outlined a game plan.

Step One: Depending on where John Doe appeared the first decent morning in February, I would alert the Vet as to what location we would be using, my property or my neighbor's. I would bang on my feeder while calling him. If he didn't come in, I'd call Mary and Dick, they'd go bang on theirs, call me right back if John Doe appeared and I'd jump in the car for the 30-second trip to their house. If he didn't come in to their feeder, I would bang on mine again and wait. I would have several blankets, a couple of towels, a water-repellent tarp, a bowl of treats and the sedative/tranquilizer shots, cotton balls and alcohol with me. Just before heading to wherever John Doe was, I'd call the Vet to tell him we'd begun the process.

Of course, this wasn't the sort of thing we could rehearse, so hope and prayer would play a big part at this juncture: that John Doe would be ready to eat right then, that he would start to eat from the feeder with intermittent teasers from his bowl of treats, that he would stand at the feeder long enough for me to give the shot, and keep eating, to give the Vet time to get there. The catch with this was, he really wasn't supposed to have any food, and for 12 hours before the procedure. There had to be a trade-off however, so the trick was going to be to really not give him much to eat at all, to drag out the bites he was offered, and at the same time make him believe he was getting his usual ration. Well, maybe those visitors from outer space would drop in for a reception after all.

Step Two: With John Doe at whichever feeder, I would give him the shot in the fleshy part of the back of a thigh. Since he faced the feeder as he ate so his hind end was exposed this should be relatively easy. I was to get the shot in him as soon as possible after I arrived, and hope that the prick and injection didn't scare him off. When living in my barn, he was such a good patient with all the shots I had to give him, but that had been some months ago. It was impossible to predict how he would react now to a shot.

The drugs recommended were Cadacet and Rompin. The deer expert at the University said this combination would work well to sedate him, and that he would get drowsy and lie down within 7-12 minutes. That sounded like a dreadfully long time to me, with an awful lot of acres to wander in the meantime if he tired of nibbling. I was to stay with him no matter what. I knew ahead that would be a time of more prayer. The dosage was 1/3 of a cc per 30mgs, though when using Cadacet, only a 1/2 dose of Rompin would be needed. With much input and help from Mary and Dick, we estimated his weight at about 70 lbs. I double-checked the estimate and math for the dosages with the deer expert prior to the Big Day.

Step Three: When John Doe began to get drowsy, and started to go down, I had to be ready to put the tarp down first, then a couple blankets on top of the tarp, directly underneath him, and then a blanket covering him. He had to have protection from damp and cold ground below him, and cold air around him. So, simultaneously as he went down, I had to quickly get the tarp and blankets underneath him, and support him as he dropped to make sure he dropped gently. I counted my hands and seemed to come up short, but we'd just have to wait until that day to see how things went.

Above all, it was important John Doe be kept warm and calm, that I be quiet and calm, and that the surroundings be the same. A towel lightly draped across his face, covering his eyes and ears, would help minimize or eliminate exterior stimulus that might startle him and counteract or slow the sedative's effectiveness.

Step Four: The Vet would arrive. John Doe would hopefully be fully sedated, and under the influence of the sedative be drifting in some 'happy place'. I would hopefully be ready for the next steps, one of which was to prop up his head and chest while he was 'out'. This is to aid breathing, and to prevent the slightest bit of pneumonia from taking hold. Anything to do with the Vet's part in all this I left to him. I knew he knew what he had to do and how to do it.

Step Five: The Vet would administer whatever anesthetic, wait the necessary time for John Doe to be fully knocked out, check his vitals, and then perform the neutering.

Step Six: This would be Aftercare and Recovery. The outdoors would have to serve as both. Obviously it would also serve as the Pre-Op, and O-R. The Vet would stay for about 20 minutes after neutering, to monitor his vitals. Then I would be on my own with him, monitoring and keeping him warm while the anesthetic began working its way out of his system. I had to continue to keep his head and chest elevated, so once I assumed that position, I would have to keep it for the duration. I would have to make sure I was as warm and comfortable as I could get before the procedure even began. Mary had told me she would bring me tea and snacks while I sat with John Doe.

So that was our plan in a nutshell. Only time and the event itself would tell if it would work, or how well it would work, or what we forgot. Between The Plan's inception and the actual day of neutering, I had several more conversations with the Vet, the deer expert at the University, and Mary and Dick, going over details and mentally rehearsing The Plan. January 30 I packed my supplies in a duffle, minus the shot which I would draw the morning of the neutering. So I was ready to roll. Roughly four years later I would use this same plan with Baby Buck. When I get to his story I'll just send you back here for a review of The Plan. It would have a few minor changes, but was essentially the same.

Chapter 13

The first four days of February came and went. They were not candidates for days on which to neuter a fawn out in the open, as they were overcast, windy and chilly. Before I digressed to tell about the neutering, we were at February 5, the day John Doe came in with the mama and fawn. That didn't seem the day to do it, although weather-wise it would have been fine. He seemed to be having such a nice time with his new friends though, I didn't want to interrupt any on-going bonding.

The next morning though, February 6, was a gorgeous sunny day, not a cloud in sight. We hadn't had snow in several days and what we had gotten had melted so the ground wouldn't be too damp. The signs were good. Now the only thing needed was the main star of the show so to speak, to arrive, at either my feeder or Mary and Dick's. I fixed the shot and went out to my feeder to bang and call for John Doe.

As luck would have it, he arrived at Mary and Dick's feeder. I would have preferred he'd been here, thinking maybe as the sedative took effect I could guide him into the barn. It would make for such a cozy O-R, and Recovery Room. I called the Vet and told him I was on my way to give the sedative at their feeder, that if all went smoothly, he would be given the shot within about five minutes. Mary and Dick would watch for the Vet to arrive and direct him to where John Doe and I were, which would be hopefully still near the feeder. The Plan was off to a good start and Step One was complete. We had our 'neuteree' cooperatively doing his command performance so to speak at a feeder. Onward to Step Two.

I grabbed the shot and duffle and drove to Mary's. I'd done this on many occasions, so he was used to seeing me arrive by car. I put a few morsels of grain in the feeder, just enough to get him started. With his first bite, I swabbed the back of his right thigh with alcohol. I waited until he was grabbing a few more morsels of grain, poked the needle in, and after aspirating, plunged in the sedative. He didn't seem to notice. Phew, done. Step Two complete.

Now began Step Three and perhaps the iffiest part: waiting for John Doe to drop and the Vet to arrive, hoping the two would be close in time, and praying John Doe would not wander far in the meantime. And I had to get the coverings down under him with split-second timing. I slowly offered him more morsels, and dragged out the giving of them. He did not wander off at all and soon the sedative began to do its work. It took 7 ½ minutes for the sedative to take effect. When he did drop we were just five feet from the feeder, in a spot half-lawn and half soft brush. Perfect. I got the tarp and blankets under him just as he dropped, and somehow at the same time helped him down gently. Say what you will, I know God was right there lending His hands. Step Three done. We were halfway through The Plan, and so far not a hitch.

The Vet arrived within a couple minutes of John Doe going down. Step Four was in progress. I had just placed a towel across his face and he was still and quiet. I slowly raised his head and chest, propping them on my thighs. The Vet walked softly and carried a big medical bag. It wasn't really big, but when a near-adage drops in your lap, you go with it, for better or worse. John Doe didn't stir at all when the Vet knelt down to begin. We had gone over the details of this so many times, that we didn't need to speak. Step Four complete.

On to Step Five. He administered the anesthetic, gave me an encouraging smile, and we waited for it to knock John Doe out. He checked his vitals which were fine. Once John Doe was totally out, he performed the neutering which took about five minutes. Step Five done. Just one Step to go.

Step Six began as planned, with the Vet staying about 20 minutes, checking and rechecking his vitals. He gave me a thumbs-up and a hug, held his hand to his ear miming a phone call, and quietly left. The Plan had worked, and everything had fallen into place. Gosh, I've neglected to give any time-frame for any of this. It was about 7:15 that morning when I got to Mary's feeder and John Doe. It was not quite 7:25 when John Doe dropped from the sedative. The Vet arrived about 7:40 and the procedure was over at about 8 am.

After he left, Aftercare and Recovery began, for me too. As promised, Mary appeared with a much-appreciated cup of tea and some snacks. In fact several times the rest of the morning she brought me goodies. Somehow it worked out that John Doe dropped close enough to a tree that I could use it as a back support for me while his head and chest were in my lap. What a help that was. I settled back to monitor John Doe and wait for him to come to. He was out cold until 12:30. My legs and arms had long since gone numb, not from any cold but from the weight, and it was 'dead' weight, of his head and chest on them for the last 4 ½ hours.

When John Doe came to, he got up a lot quicker and more nimbly than I did. He was also steadier on his feet sooner than I was. While I was still rubbing my legs and arms to get the circulation going, he was walking into the woods. When I caught up with him, he was nibbling on some vegetation. He was still a bit groggy, and after a few minutes he fratched around in one spot like deer, and dogs, do just before they lie down. Fortunately I'd thought to grab the blankets and tarp and got them under him just in the nick of time.

For another couple of hours he just rested in the classic deer pose with his four legs folded underneath him, his head resting on a foreleg. The next time he got up, he was totally steady on his feet, his eyes were clear, and the grogginess was gone. It seemed Step Six was complete.

He headed back in the direction of my property so I walked the path with him. When he headed into the woods just below my barn and lay down, I felt he was recovered well enough to leave him. I did put the tarp and blankets underneath him, and a blanket on top of him.

Then I walked back to Mary and Dick's to retrieve my supplies and thank them for all their help, then drove home. I could see John Doe from the windows on the back side of the house, so throughout the rest of the day I watched him.

About 5 pm he came to my back deck and looked in the sliding glass door to the room where I happened to be sitting. I took out a bowl with a little water and just a few bites of grain and treats. He was still doing fine. He headed back to the same spot below my barn and lay down again. He had come through the procedure and out of the anesthetic so well that I felt confident he would be fine overnight.

Considering all the variables involved in his neutering and The Plan, most stemming from the fact that he was a fawn in the wild, the timing of things that could have gone awry and didn't, the unexpected that could have occurred and didn't, it was remarkable how smoothly every part went. That was a real blessing, and as with so much of his raising and care, this too had been a team effort. 'Thank you God, for bringing all this together, and watching over John Doe throughout the process.'

Chapter 14

February 7, the morning after his neutering, was another beautifully clear and fairly nice day for winter. It was barely light when I awakened and went to the barn to feed the horses. Half an hour later and now full daylight, as I was coming out of the barn, something caught my attention out of the corner of my eye. I turned, and trotting across the field to me was John Doe. What a sight! He was obviously fully recovered from the anesthetic and procedure, feeling good, and ready for breakfast.

I obliged as quickly as I could, running inside and tossing grain and treats in his bowl while he waited patiently outside my back deck. I didn't give him a full bowl, only about half his normal ration, as the Vet had said to go easy on food the next day. He ate what I offered and seemed content with that. He was in three more times that day, and I skipped every other meal of treats. In between times, he would browse a little, then return to the spot below the barn.

Over the next several days when he came in, he was once again in the company of mama and her young ones, and I was delighted to see he'd reconnected with them after his procedure. Beyond these days, more often than not when he came in, it was with his 'family'. Like Lone Fawn, he would leave them to come get his treats. Like her, sometimes they would leave and he'd stay for awhile, other times he'd leave with them. His group, like hers, seemed like a family. There was much interaction, deer-style. Lots of nuzzling went on between all of them which was cute to watch.

John Doe and the button-buck and his sister would play, chasing each other around the fields, sometimes running into my back yard and circling the house. The pace was break-neck, but I was reminded how important this play is in developing muscles, leg strength, agility and stamina, which some day could mean the difference between life and death. It was like watching a living miracle to see him race at these high speeds and be so agile, this fawn that was once so sickly, near death, with a broken leg.

Though John Doe had not and most likely would not develop antlers, his testosterone level must have remained high enough that he and his button-buck 'brother' knew he was still basically a buck, because the button buck, with even just his little nubbins of antlers, would try to engage him in the antler play that bucks often do. There are times when it is not play between the big boys, for example, during mating season, or when a strange buck intrudes on another's territory. It can be deadly serious then. But so often it is just play, and fine-tuning their skills for using their antlers in defense or offense, which as adults they might one day have to do.

These two 'boys' were kids however, and their jousting was all in play. What was remarkable to me was that John Doe seemed to know what it was all about, what to do and how to do it, and he went through the motions even though he didn't have so much as a hint of antlers. In essence, he was pretending, play-acting, playing a role that genetics had programmed into him and his brain, whether he had the outward actual 'equipment' or not. Perhaps more remarkable, the button buck somehow knew that John Doe was a buck despite no buttons or antlers and being neutered. [whether that gave off any scent or vibes, who knows?] In any case, in each other's eyes they were both just young bucks, and as such, it was 'time to rumble'. I always regretted not videoing these play times, the general play between John Doe and his 'siblings', but more especially the antler play-jousting between John Doe and the button buck.

So throughout February and into March, John Doe was still coming in several times a day. There were some days when he wouldn't be in until late night around 11. I'd usually be in the barn, spending time with the horses, grooming them or mucking stalls.

You know how you get a feeling that someone's watching you though you've not yet seen anyone? That feeling would come, I'd look out from a stall or turn around, and there would be John Doe standing looking at me. He'd usually follow me as I headed to the house, for his treats, and for some patting and nuzzles.

Through the first two weeks of March he was in practically every day at least twice a day, still traveling with his family. Though I think there were times past this date when I saw him, the last date I actually noted him being in was March 13. Sitting here today I do recall that I did get reports from folks in the neighborhoods nearby, and from Mary and Dick, or other of my neighbors, that they'd seen John Doe, on such and such days or dates, how he looked and what he was doing. That yellow tag made him so easy to spot and recognize.

There were other folks who lived in adjacent neighborhoods with whom I'd not spoken, who'd heard about him from their friends or neighbors, and they'd call me with news of him. It's funny how memories work isn't it? As I write and reflect, more and more comes back to me about this. It became a sort of neighborhood-watch program, thought it wasn't crime or criminals folks were on the lookout for, but a fawn, soon to be a yearling, named John Doe, with a bright yellow tag in his ear.

I remember some parents telling me that he was becoming a sort of legend in their neighborhood, and what glee it brought their kids to be able to say that THEY had seen John Doe. Then they'd want to hear the story about him. Some of these parents hadn't heard any of the story, so they'd ask if I minded filling them in, which of course I didn't. I also remember at least one child calling me himself to say he'd seen John Doe, and asked me "where'jou get this deer anyway?" So I told him John Doe's story, and he loved it.

While March 13 was the last date I noted that he was in, I know I continued to see him beyond that on and off, not only for months, but into the following year, though not with regularity. There is an explanation in that he may have moved his territory. This would account for his just passing through or near my property on his way to his new stomping grounds, and for my only occasional and infrequent sightings of him.

Spring and fawning season were just around the bend. With Spring's arrival imminent, and fawning to soon follow in May, pregnant does become focused almost exclusively on feeding themselves in preparation for delivery of their offspring, to maintain their own body weight and fat, but also for the nutritional needs of their unborn. Just before delivery, they drive away all other deer, including their year-old fawns. After the births, sometime in mid-summer, mamas welcome back their female yearlings into the fold. Whether she does this with her male yearlings isn't a given or known for certain.

It may be that the opportunity to issue such an invitation doesn't present itself, because having been driven off by their mamas just prior to her delivering, yearling bucks often take off on exploratory jaunts that may take them into totally new and distant territories. They may remain there and adopt these new grounds as their new home one. So it could well be that when John Doe and his button-buck 'sibling' were driven off by mama, they ended up traveling far away and settled in a new territory some distance from here, but one that still overlapped with his old territory, my property and our hilltop.

Whenever my last sighting of John Doe was, knowing that he would not develop antlers and therefore wouldn't be a trophy for hunters remained a huge comfort to me. Just as comforting, on a personal level, was knowing that if he were still with me and in our neighborhood in the next two to three years, he would be the same sweet gentleman with me that he always had been, and not a raving maniac trying to kill me. Those thoughts stayed with me I'm sure and reassured me about his future, whether I had gotten to see or spend time with him again or not.

While we never got to say a formal goodbye, John Doe and I, that was all right. Getting to say a goodbye is not always a good thing in some ways, as I was to find out later. In retrospect, then and now, while he was here, I had done my best, with much help from so many others, to get him fixed up for a fresh start in life. When he was released, I had done my best, again with much help, to bolster and protect him, for the long as well as the short term. In the times since then, and since my final sighting of him, I preferred to imagine him in his new territory, doing what deer do, healthy and fit enough to do it, and being content, secure, and happy enjoying life in the wild.

As my friend said in his note, I had indeed been given a beautiful, delicate gift. Here was a little wild creature, who endured so many traumas -- the loss of his mama, a broken leg, life-threatening digestive problems, and neutering; who tolerated more human hands-on and intervention than probably 99% of any fawns ever hand-raised; and who accepted it all with an undaunted spirit and gentle heart. Such a sweetheart, a brave little boy, my first, my trooper -- John Doe.

Part III
Baby Buck – My Fixture

Chapter 1

It was another five years before the next foundling fawn came into my life, Saturday May 21, 1994. About 7 pm, five pounds of dots, spots, and speckled fur, with four long spindly legs and a tiny body attached, was delivered to my house by a fellow in a small pick-up truck. It was through calling different Vets in the area and landing on mine - -the one who had hooked me up with John Doe years earlier - - that this fellow was referred to me. He called asking if he could bring a little male fawn to me. Hmm, let's see -- To raise a fawn or not raise a fawn -- what a silly question. It would be about 40 minutes before he got here. I had much to do.

I went to the barn to share the news with the horses. I swear it looked like they rolled their eyes at each other. Maybe it was my imagination. Really I went to the barn to prepare a stall with fresh cushy bedding, put out a bowl of water, and get the netting out and nailed up across the stall openings.

Bothered by my hammering in one of their stalls, the horses headed to the far pasture, glaring at me as they passed by. Well, it looked like a glare. Maybe I hadn't imagined their rolling eyes after all. I closed off the other stall and run-in shed. I would make sure to give them extra treats later, and throughout the little one's stay. [note to self: stock up on apples] The last barn prep was to make sure the radio was on and set to a quiet music station.

At the house I gathered my baby animal supplies: bottles, nipples, cotton balls, towels, thermometer, scales, and a pen and notebook. I was at the sink washing and sterilizing bottles and nipples, so excited about another fawn to help, feeling very organized and ready, and with time to spare, when it suddenly hit me - - MILK! I need milk! Not just milk -- GOAT'S milk.

Crossing my fingers and saying a quick prayer that she still had goats, and still milked them, heck that she even still lived here, I called the girl who'd been my milk supplier for John Doe. She *was* still here, still "in the business" and had a supply of fresh milk in the fridge. I was there, giving new meaning and a much later hour to the phrase "milk run", in 5 minutes, and home in 10. Just before 7 pm I was putting the milk in the fridge when I heard the truck coming up the drive. I remember saying "Baby Buck has arrived!"

He was half-asleep, lying quietly in the driver's lap. It wasn't until the guy got out with the folded-up bundle in his arms, that the darling face, with its soft brown eyes, dark nose, and sweet expression, and the graceful head with its antenna-like ears, became visible. He was so adorable. He was so tiny. Like John Doe, this one's mama had been killed by a car and he too needed a jump start and lots of TLC.

The fellow now carrying the fawn to my barn explained it was he who had hit the mama, and how terribly he felt. When he saw the fawn standing motionless next to its mama, staring down at her, he was afraid at first that it too had been hit. As far as he could tell though, it had not. It was probably confused, surely in shock emotionally, and afraid. Not giving the fawn any time to bolt, he quickly scooped him up, climbed into his truck and put the fawn on his lap. He said his next thought was: "Harry, you live in an apartment -- what in hell are you gonna do with a fawn?!" That's when he thought of calling Vets. He then told me how the little thing was shaking when he first picked it up and put it on his lap, but had calmed down very quickly, and for the rest of the trip rode in his lap as quietly as any of his dogs. Remorse at hitting and killing a deer, saving its fawn, dogs, and dogs riding in his lap in the car -- this guy was my kind o' folk.

He carried him into the stall and gently set him down. For several minutes the fawn stood frozen in place, looking from me to the guy and the guy to me, back and forth several times. I knelt down and began talking softly to him. "Baby Buck" had just blurted out of me at the fridge, so since he'd apparently been dubbed, I started using his name right away. I told him who I was, that he'd be staying here for awhile until he was a little older and stronger, and able to be on his own, and that then he'd be released.

This beautiful tiny creature looked up at me as I spoke, as if he were not only paying attention, but understanding what I was saying. No, no hyper-anthropomorphism here, I know he wasn't understanding-understanding what I was saying. It's just the way he was holding eye contact with me as he listened, that lent the impression that something was registering in his brain. What he was grasping I think, was that I was a friend, that for now anyway this new place was home, and that it was a safe place. He began to look and walk around the stall, scanning the scene. He was calm and began to relax more and more, until finally he lay down. That seemed a good time to walk the guy back to his truck.

I waited for a bit then warmed a bottle and went to see if Baby Buck was interested in some milk. He wasn't. Not in the least. In fact, he would turn his head away from it. Now either he really wasn't hungry, or he just didn't know what this bottle contraption was and didn't particularly like it being moved toward his face and mouth. Or perhaps despite his outwardly calm demeanor, he was still stressed from the day's ordeals of losing his mama, his truck ride, and finding himself in this enclosure.

I'd raised only one fawn and he'd immediately grabbed the bottle and started gulping with such gusto that he'd just about bowled me over. So this was, well, different. He'll eat when he's hungry, I thought, and sat down near him so we could get better acquainted -- which we did, and fairly fast. I'd kept skooching closer and closer to him, until I was right beside him, and kept talking to him. He watched me intently, but didn't seem to mind the proximity. I started patting him, and stroking his fur starting at the top of his head and going all the way to his tail.

As I write this, June 20, 2007, there is a fawn bleating somewhere around my front yard and the woods near it. It would be irony to have this occur as I write about my fawns if it were unusual still to have fawns and deer regularly on my property. But it isn't [unusual], so it's not [irony]. Anyway, I'm pretty sure it's the little one whose mama has been leaving it each day for the past two weeks in my 'Day Care' front field. Sometimes it gets impatient if mama's not yet back. It leaves its bedding spot, runs around bleating for a little, then settles in another spot, and waits again for mama. Mama shows up every day, but not until about 4 pm. Each day if I'm home and hear it, I call to it, tell it to relax, find a spot, and that mama *will* be back.

Chapter 2

Back to Baby Buck and our first hours together. As I was stroking him down the length of his little body, he got more and more relaxed, until finally, his head and neck dropped onto my lap. This little boy was relaxed to the max. I think the stress of the events of the day had caught up to him, and he was just plum tuckered out. Once again I had a little fawn's weight on my thighs and lap for an extended time, as he stayed in that position for a good 45 minutes.

I know what you're thinking: he was only five pounds. True. But having to stay frozen in one place, without moving a muscle, no matter how small the weight pressing on whatever anatomical part, things start to go numb. At least my things start to go numb. I didn't dare move because I thought it would startle him, and I didn't want to cause him one more upset for the day. It worked out all right though as I ended up having a nice little rest, despite the tingly thing going on.

When he did rouse, he did so without any fanfare. He just slowly sat up, then stood up. I had to work a bit to wake up those sleepy legs attached to me. I thought maybe he was hungry, so I went to get a fresh bottle. Nope, still not hungry. It was about 9 pm by then, with daylight coming to a close. I had the horses to hay, and my dogs to let outside, so I went to take care of and spend time with them.

One important thing that went well from the beginning was getting him to go to the bathroom. As described in John Doe's story, I had to 'play mama', and use the warm wet cotton balls. After just two days, and getting tinkled on only once or twice when my reflexes were slow, he was going on his own. That category got a big check mark on my benchmark list, and he got a gold star, May 25. But back to that first day.

I'd decided that I would offer him a bottle every two to three hours. Once he took his first bottle, we'd start our every-four-hour schedule of feedings. Surely by midnight he would be hungry. As I'd done with John Doe, I began talking and saying "hi" whenever I approached the barn. Midnight came and went, as did 2:30 am, and 5 am, with no interest from him in milk. A couple of the times I went out I think I even woke him. I was glad someone was getting some sleep. I was beginning to be concerned at his lack of hunger, but decided that come morning, well, later morning, he'd be chomping at the bit for milk. With that thought, I crawled into bed again, having decided that he would not starve if I slept for a much-needed stretch.

Around 9:30 am I awoke. Trying not to think about how off-schedule my horses and dogs now were, let alone me, [I never sleep that late], I fixed a bottle. When I got to his stall, he was lying quietly. I thought it might peak his interest and help him get revved up for milk, if I didn't go to him right away, so I fed the horses their grain and hay. Then I went into the stall. He came over to greet me, which was so cute. He was nuzzling me all over, surely saying "got milk?" As I held out the bottle and tried to put it in his mouth, it wasn't "got milk" at all, it was "no way josé ". Well, what do we do now?, I thought. He'd been without sustenance or nutrition for at least sixteen-plus hours. I called my deer expert friends at our zoo, brought them up to date, and asked their advice. They told me exactly what to do and how to do it, although as I listened, I could not really believe I would be able to do what they described, or that it would work. I was good at "Twister" as a kid, but I was a lot older now and this sounded like a job for - - TA DA! SUPER-CONTORTIONIST! "Nothing ventured, nothing gained" came to mind and I became determined that I would make this work. After all, how strong could a five-pound fawn be? Funny you should ask.

I went into the stall and assumed 'The Position': down on my knees, sitting on my haunches with my heels underneath and knees spread, setting the bottle in the sawdust beside me. I was ready to follow the directions for the game, er, procedure, which I called: "How Many Hands Does It Take To Fold A Fawn?"

It goes like this: when he came to me, with an arm and hand on each of his sides and shoulders, [I don't know about you, but that seemed to call for four arms and hands, already using up all mine and putting me "in the red" before we'd even begun], I was to turn him around, and guide and pull him backwards, gently but firmly, between my spread-out knees; closing my knees and using them, my upper body and arms to hold him in place, again gently but firmly, [that seemed to call for at least another two arms and hands, at a minimum -- so now I needed, what? six?], one by one I was to fold up each of his small legs under him, [now, exactly how many of the six hands and arms already committed to his sides, shoulders, and holding him in place, would I be able to borrow from their already-designated tasks to accomplish this folding-up maneuver? Sounded to me like robbing Peter to pay Paul, when Peter was already having trouble making ends meet], making him into a compact and manageable package -- the operative word being "manageable"; then, leaning my upper body against his back at the same time that I brought the bottle to his mouth with one hand, I was to use my other hand to get the bottle into his mouth however much prying it might take. [definitely another two hands called for -- making a grand total of eight.] Do I even need to say that it was not easy and that it did not go smoothly? And did I mention I don't *have* eight hands?

He did not just let me do his. In fact he fought it, all 5 pounds of him against my 110. Remember what you read earlier about how much more muscle fiber-per-lb deer have than humans? Well, I hadn't. Or I thought it applied only to adult deer. Think again Einstein. Granted, the ratios are probably considerably smaller with one as little as this, but he was mighty none the less.

Not only mighty, he was wiry and wily. I'd get two legs folded, and be going for the third, when he'd get one or both of the first ones unfolded. I'd get three folded, and think we were practically home free, only to have him get one, two, or even three of the three, *un*folded, just as I was getting the fourth folded, and here we go again.

It was like trying to nail jell-o to the wall. Actually, I felt I would have had better odds with the jell-o. At least it didn't have a mind of its own. That fellow Atlas, or was it Sisyphus? who had to roll that ball of fire, or was it a boulder? up a hill for eternity, kept coming to mind. Whichever fellow it was, I'm sure he would have had Baby Buck neatly folded up the day before he even began the task.

Finally, a half hour and five or six folding-unfolding bouts later, Baby Buck had a bottle in his mouth and was drinking! Unfortunately, he drank only 2 ½ oz that first time. What was it Churchill said?: never have so few done so much for so little? That's not it, but it'll do. I dreaded the thought of having to go more 'rounds' with him over the bottle, without at least a bench-press training session or two, but the deer expert said that once he realized that this thing, the bottle, had milk in it, it would be a breeze. Bring on the breezes, I was exhausted, and hot.

The next feeding wasn't a breeze, but it was close. Halfway through the folding process, he gave in, and I didn't even have to pry open his mouth. He took another 3 oz. He was definitely a slow starter, but at least he'd left the gate. Four hours later, he took 5 oz. We had to do the folding process each of those times, but each time it got easier and each time he gave in sooner, and my back, legs, arms, and every muscle in them, could be heard sighing 'THANK you'. The last feeding was at 11 pm. As I entered the stall, he was actually looking for the bottle. No more calls, we HAVE a winner! He drank another 5 oz. Though he'd had slightly less than half of the 32 oz daily requirement, things were looking up. I was looking for a hot bath, and a night's sleep.

One last word about this 'Fold-a-Fawn' procedure. The way a deer normally lies down mimics this exactly. They fold up rather like a card table, one leg at a time, beginning with the front legs one at a time, then a back leg, then as the fourth leg folds, they drop with a plop. I'd seen Baby Buck do this on his own, so it wasn't that he didn't know how. It must have been that he didn't like someone forcing him to do it. What was your first clue, Sherlock?

I didn't take many photos of Baby Buck in his stall in the beginning. In the one below he's loose in the barn, and it was taken after he'd been here about ten days.

Actually, after searching and searching, and not finding all that many photos of him compared to the other fawns, in particular those with key moments, I finally remembered that for a year and a half, I didn't have a good still camera. The only one I had was a Polaroid that took lousy photos. Even it must have been on the blink in 1995 as I have no photos of Baby Buck for that whole year. I do have videos galore of him-in the barn, beside the barn, ambling in for his bowl, walking onto the deck, walking off the deck, in the front yard.... . On those videos are some key moments that I kept hunting for among the stills.

Chapter 3

Monday morning dawned into one of those perfect Spring mornings, clear, crisp and sunny -- just downright beautiful. I'd awakened refreshed about 5, made over my dogs, fed and let them outside for a romp. Next, to the horses. I'd moved their grain buckets, normally in their stalls, to the fence behind the barn. I gave them a little extra grain, threw in a couple apples, then threw some hay out for them. No rolling eyes or glares --I'd been forgiven. I think the apples did it. [memo to self: keep the apples coming] I opened up the pastures for them. Only then did I get a bottle and go see my little 'charge'. I hoped he remembered that he now just took the bottle without any wrangling. He did, and we never had to go another 'round'.

When I entered the barn he was wide awake, and waiting for me just inside the stall door. He went for the bottle excitedly but respectfully and didn't half-maul me as John Doe used to do. He still took 'The Stance', firmly planted, and guzzled with gusto, but it wasn't overbearing. In fact, with Baby Buck, I never even almost fell over once! I was coming up in the world.

That Monday morning, he took 5 ½ oz right off the bat. At Noon, he took 7 -- his record so far. At 5 pm, he took 6 and at 10:30 pm he took 4. 22 ½ oz for the day! Another 10 and we'd be at the daily required amount. The next two days he took 24, evenly spread out with 6 oz each feeding. The next day was 27 and the day after that, 28. [This is sounding like those old SAT puzzles: Train A leaves Boston at 6 am, doing 110 mph, heading due South for 43 miles, then Southwest for 56 miles; Train B leaves Philly at 10 am, at 88 mph, heading due North for 61 miles, then Northeast for 37 miles-how long before they collide? I never *could* figure those out -- the only answer I ever came up with was, fire the track-coordinator who was obviously incompetent, but it was never even one of the choices.]

I weighed him and he'd doubled his weight in just five days and was now a whopping 11 lbs. We hit a plateau of 28 oz for four days. Beginning May 30 he had his first 32 oz day, and that continued until the day he was released -- and beyond, as you'll later read. I noted that June 6 he weighed 16 lbs, but that's the last weight notation I made.

There were no digestive problems with Baby Buck. He didn't need any meds or shots. He had no injuries or broken bones with which either he or I had to contend. Other than a slightly contentious start getting him to take the bottle, he was such an easy keeper. He lived in my barn from May 21 through July 17, and we never had one emergency. He was so easy that the few times when I had appointments and had to ask friends for feeding help -- yes, Sally again, and my sister Mary Paull -- Baby Buck was an equal opportunity bottle drinker. 'No need for any formalities, just my bottle and treats please.'

Some of his antics not only as a fawn but an adult too, used to make me chuckle a lot. Replaying some of them today in writing about them has me chuckling again. Whenever I opened his stall door to go in or out, I only opened it just enough for me to slide in sideways. Many times he'd be waiting for his bottle just inside the stall door and when I opened it and slid in, in his excitement and enthusiasm, he ran out. The first time it happened I almost panicked, as the main barn doors to 'freedom' were open, but somehow I didn't. He skidded to a stop, outside the stall door, wheeled around and looked at me over the stall door. Knowing something was wrong with this picture, me with the milk being where he was *not*, but not knowing exactly how to remedy the situation [that first time anyway] -- how to come around the edge of the door and find the opening into the stall -- he just stood there with his head cocked, like 'ahem, *some*one's in the wrong place'.

I frantically started calling him, [remember I was one baby step away from panic mode], slid my arm holding the bottle through the door opening and waved it to get his attention, then used it to lure him through the door opening. From that first time on whenever this same thing happened, it took him mere seconds to find the opening and get back into the stall. No match for Algernon maybe, [remember that smart little mouse who ran the mazes in the Cliff Robertson movie "Charly"?], but a respectable showing.

I've neglected to mention that we guessed, the local deer experts and I, that Baby Buck was born sometime around May 14, 15, or 16, give or take one or two days. So when he came to me, he was just 1 week old at the most. No wonder he was so tiny. John Doe had been about 3 to 4 weeks old and weighed fifteen to twenty pounds when he came. Where Baby Buck was calm, cool and collected, well, save those first bouts with me and the bottle, John Doe, while he definitely had his calm, snuggly moments, was 'feisty'; perhaps because of all with which he had to contend, he had to be a 'fighter' to make it through all he did. Baby Buck sort of breezed through without a 'hitch in the get-a-long'.

As I'd done with John Doe, I took to opening up his stall door, after making sure the other stall door to the run-in shed and the main barn doors were shut, to let him walk about in the barn, get some exercise and start building up his muscles. He enjoyed it immensely. Then one day, out of the blue, he startled the heck out of me when he began an aerobics program all on his own. He suddenly took off like a bat, and began doing laps in the barn. He would take off running from one stall corner, race out the door, dart into the other stall, run into its corner, wheel around and head back out the stall door, all in high gear. He not only ran during these laps, at times he leapt.

At first I was a little hesitant about his doing all this, worried that he might misjudge distance and run smack into a wall or something. He never did, but was as agile and accurate as a ballerina as he raced around the barn. Sometimes he would jump onto the first layer of hay bales in the course of a lap, never miss a beat, jump off and continue the lap. Clearly his legs were strong and getting stronger.

He would cease his aerobics as suddenly as he had begun, and stop right in front of me, a little winded. He'd stand there for a few moments, catch his breath and look at me, as if to say, "pretty good, eh?" This always made me smile, but then so much he did had that effect. This had been true with John Doe, and would be true of the other fawns to come, but with Baby Buck there was an extra something from the beginning.

In another few moments, he'd begin nuzzling me, or my book or tea mug, looking for something to eat or drink. So I'd go to the house and get him a little something, or if it were meal-time I'd bring it to him. Often by the time I returned, he'd be in his stall having a drink of water or a lick at his salt block, or lying down resting.

Chapter 4

In June and July, my sister came frequently with her two sons, eight and five years old. These were aside from times she occasionally filled in for me at feeding times. I'm sure they came to see me, in part. But I didn't just get off the boat -- I know the main drawing card was Baby Buck. The boys loved getting to feed him, or just hang out with him in his stall or if he was loose in the barn. Below, Shawn is giving him bites of carrot.

They also continued to come after his release, and helped give him his bottles then as well. They were pretty amazed at getting to be so up close and personal with what was now a 'wild' animal, or at least one who was living in the wild, yet still get to feed and pat him. They were more amazed when they'd visit, and I'd call him, and Baby Buck would come running from wherever he was. They used to laugh and say "he comes like he's a DOG!" 'Out of the mouths of babes... .' Here, Timothy is holding his own against 'the stance'.

June and July went by uneventfully, other than that we had beautiful weather all month, with very few storms or bad weather. If it rained, it seemed to come overnight, and the next day would be dry and clear. I put up the wire enclosure I'd used with John Doe, and began letting him out in it during the day. He loved it. He'd spend hours out there, basking in the sun, watching the horses graze, or watching deer pass through the fields. I always wondered, as I had with John Doe, did they know they were looking at their own kind? He was obviously smart and 'street-savvy' as on extra-hot or humid days, he went back in the barn where it was cooler, and the ceiling fan was going.

Earlier in the book I mentioned about deer play, how the invitation-to-play from a deer is the same as with puppies and dogs. They lower their heads, bobbing them back and forth, and bring their chests low, almost to the ground. Then they sort of weave their hind ends back and forth, while hopping back and forth, side-to-side or forward and backward.

The first time Baby Buck invited me to play, I thought he was having some sort of fit, or had something stuck in his throat. I knew from books what it looked like, and knew from watching Lone Fawn with other fawns, or other deer and bucks doing it, but I'd obviously forgotten. When I finally remembered, and was so relieved he didn't have something wrong, I got such a kick out of being asked to play by a little fawn. I did the best I could, not being a fawn and all. And I must have passed muster as he'd keep going, and he and I would bob and dance around the stall, heads and fannies weaving back and forth.

He may have been just humoring me, who knows? I thought it was great fun, but was always the one who stopped first. I hoped he at least gave me an "E" for effort, as I stood there heaving, trying to catch my breath. Into adulthood, and over the years, he still invited me to play at times, and that always made me feel I'd been made an honorary deer of sorts.

Two friends of mine ran a Christian Day-Care that summer, and wanted to do a field trip here to meet Baby Buck. July 1, they arrived with six little three-and four-year-olds in tow. Since this audience was on the whole younger than John Doe's, I revamped my spiel and kept it very simple -- telling what and how old he was, his name, what he liked to eat.

I told them he might suddenly take off running around the barn, that that was ok, not to be afraid, and not to scream or yell. "Blah Blah Blah" may be all they actually heard, but I counted on their 'keepers' to manage them, which they did. So the little ones filed in, holding each others' hands, with my friends holding their little hands. Quiet as mice, they sat down on the bales of hay just where they were told.

I'd gone ahead and was kneeling next to Baby Buck in the stall, with the stall door wide open so he could see what was happening. He was good as gold too, and just stood there quietly. I walked out of the stall with him, and went over and sat down with the kids. As if on cue, Baby Buck walked over to each one to say 'Hi', sniffing their legs and arms and hands. He sniffed one little girl's neck and face, and she just grinned from ear to ear. Then he proceeded to do that with every child. He knew how to play to this crowd, and he was a hit!

There was one little boy who was sort of gruff, or maybe too 'cool' [at FOUR?!], who wasn't as enthralled as his buddies with this little creature, at first. Another few sniffs from Baby Buck though, his façade melted and he finally cracked a smile. From then on he grinned as much as the other kids.

It's no wonder that we're finally catching on to the therapeutic effect animals have on humans. Showman to the end, Baby Buck topped off their visit with his laps, the big finale, which really wowed the kids. How he missed clipping a leg or arm or two, I've no idea, because he cut it close as he leapt on and off the bales of hay so near them. But miss them he did, and did as precisely choreographed a routine as if Balanchine himself had rehearsed him. What a show-off he was! What a proud 'mama' he had!

I'd stayed in touch with the local deer experts, keeping them updated on Baby Buck's progress. They advised that if all continued to go well I should aim to release him mid-July, when he'd be about eight weeks, or two months, old. Remember that is the age when a fawn in the wild will normally begin to go with mama as she travels the routes in her territory. By that age, it is strong enough, not only to keep up, but to flee from predators. The fawn will travel with mama, mimicking her activities and learning from her about browsing and feeding, resting and bedding, dangers and flight, and where her territory boundaries are. It will learn all this at mama's side.

In Baby Buck's case, being released at this young an age would provide more of an opportunity and chance that he might be semi-adopted by, or at least allowed to tag along with, a mama and her fawns. He would then hopefully be able to learn from them all he needed to know to be a deer. Since Lone Fawn and John Doe had each been fortunate along these lines, and when 'adopted' were even older and considerably bigger than Baby Buck, it seemed he might have an even better chance at 'adoption' considering his smaller size and younger age. Surely a mama doe would recognize him as a very young one who could really use some guidance and friends, perhaps even a mama-figure.

Chapter 5

Mid-July was fast approaching. Those bittersweet feelings were reappearing. I knew it would be hard for me, but knew too that his release was a must, and felt good that he was fit, strong, and in excellent health. He was also laid-back, smart, and independent enough, so that if not adopted, I felt he would fare fine. I also knew that whatever happened, I would be available to supplement his food if necessary.

Actually, the deer experts had told me that if at all possible, and unless I saw some mama letting him nurse from her which would be a rarity, I should continue bottle feedings for at least two or more months, with supplements of carrots and grain. Of course that would depend on whether he ever came around after release. The issue of releasing him un-neutered didn't arise, with him being still so young. There was plenty of time to plan that.

I randomly chose July 17 for his release, and unless some horrendous weather came or was on the horizon, I planned to do it after his late afternoon bottle at 5:30, thinking -- no, who am I kidding? -- hoping that that way, he might come back for his late-evening one. Little did I know, nor could I have foreseen at the time, what would transpire. At the time, I just didn't have the knowledge, or enough knowledge, all in one lobe in my brain. And it wasn't only my brain that was involved, but my heart, big-time. In hindsight, the cause and effect of what did come about are very clear, and understandable.

Except for the few occasions when I had to get a pinch-hitting bottle-feeder, and there were only three or four, it was just me and Baby Buck, together every day for two months straight. They weren't just any two months, [after all, John Doe had been with me the same length of time], but the two most impressionable months in his young life, since he was just about one week old when he came to me. Remember that a fawn's first two weeks are spent virtually alone, with only brief visits from mama, just long enough for her to feed it, stimulate it to go to the bathroom, clean and groom it, and lead it to a fresh bedding spot.

Remember too that it takes the fawn roughly two weeks, a bit longer than mama's same process toward him, to imprint and bond with her, and that therefore it's these first two weeks of its life when it's most at risk of being attracted to any larger moving object. Of course, with an orphan in captivity, this 'risk' morphs into the safety of a surrogate mama. So in his very brief time with his mama for only his first week of life, even if she'd come to him twice each day, they'd only been together about 12 times -- not long enough for him to have forged a concrete bond with her. In essence and reality, he had come to see me as his true mama.

From my point of view, intellectually and heart-wise, which increased in understanding over the years, an extraordinary bond developed between us. For his part, based on his age when he came and all the rest explained above, his bonding with and imprinting on me was the natural unfolding of events, and our close relationship the natural outcome of that. So my heart needn't have been concerned he wouldn't return for his last feeding that night of his release. He was in pretty much like clockwork, at 10:30 pm. And it was far from his last feeding. From then on, and for the next four years, he was here every day, at least twice a day and sometimes more, sometimes all day, which explains why in the Prologue I give him the moniker of "my fixture" -- it was totally fitting. What my nephews said *was* prophetic -- it *was* just like having another dog.

In case the reader is now thinking, 'oh Lord, we're not *really* going to have to wade day by day through those next four years, or 1460 days, are we? Not that it might not be interesting mind you, but...the grass will be growing soon and we so love to watch that.' No dear reader. I wouldn't want to lose you now, [especially if there is just one of you, my read*er*], so you will be relieved to know that I am not going to give a daily accounting of those next four years or 1460 days with Baby Buck. We'd be here all day, right? I will hit just the highlights. Promise.

Not that those days were mundane in any way or sense of the word, because to me each day was remarkable, exceptional, extraordinary and unforgettable. But for the most part, my days with him became so routine and habitual, so much like having another pet and member of the family, [who just happened to live outside], that aside from the fact that he was a deer, there were not a lot of remarkable moments, other than the most obvious of all -- which is that he was a deer who was here at least twice a day, every day, and often all day, for four straight years. To try to relate all those many days would become so repetitious I *would* lose you .

So while my times with him were more numerous and covered a longer period of time than those with Lone Fawn or John Doe, while my connection with him was deeper and stronger on all levels, and while my notes on him are more complete, his actual written story may end up to be shorter than the others.

The following is a visual aid of sorts. It is two pages from my appointment book/ quasi-diary for the first week of August 1994. [Yes I save everything. I may not be able to find it when I need it, but if I ever had it, I still have it -- somewhere!] It will give you an idea of just how frequently he was here for just these seven days. If you really want, you can do the math to figure how many times he was in, but in essence, perusing these seven days and multiplying it by 1460, you've pretty much got his schedule, and therefore mine, for those four years.

One notation in particular instantly brings the moment back to me, and has me chuckling at his antics once again. It's the entry for early morning August 2: "Baby Buck here-ran up steps with me and pups!!" I was fostering several small puppies and had taken them

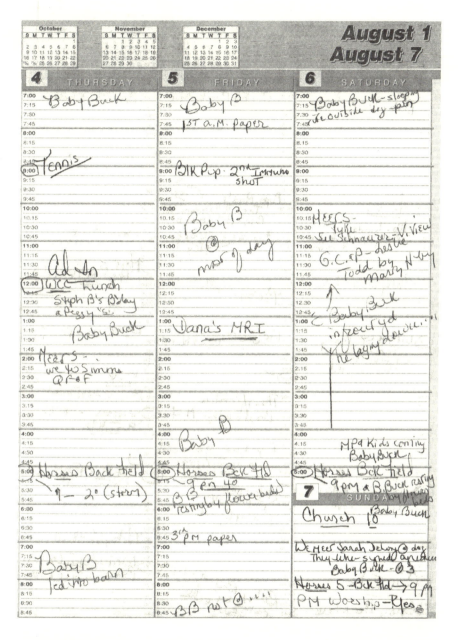

outside to go to the bathroom. When Baby Buck strolled over and began sniffing them, they bee-lined it up the steps and back onto the deck, certain that they had escaped 'the spotted beast'. Surprise -- Baby Buck had followed us right up the steps and onto the deck!

Chapter 6

So, back to Release Day, July 17. It was a perfect weather day, no storms in sight for days. I tried to bolster myself emotionally throughout the day in preparation for his leaving. Remember, I didn't know then what I came to know -- that he wasn't going anywhere, for any length of time, on any day, for the next four years. In between taking care of my horses and dogs, I spent the day with him, either in the stall, barn or fenced area outside the main barn doors. We had a lovely time.

The late-afternoon, and in my mind at the time perhaps final feeding time, came all too quickly for me. I was half-crying as I gave him his 'last' bottle, and 'last' bowl of carrots and grain. At one point, mid-bottle, he stopped drinking and licked my cheek where a few tears were running. You tell me....? I had, and have, a couple of theories, but just looked at it as one more clincher of the extraordinary bond between us. If nothing else, it 'let loose the tide', which was very cathartic. He finished his bottle and bowl of treats. It was time.

I opened up the fence enclosure. I rolled it and stashed it in the barn. He followed me into the barn. Gosh, was I going to be put to the test and have to push this one out of the nest so to speak? I took a deep breath in preparation, and walked back outside. He was right beside me again, heeling as well as any dog I'd ever had. I was talking with him the whole time as I always did. Then I headed up into the field, my little shadow in tow.

There were a few does milling around in the back field within his view, and he within theirs. But nobody seemed to notice anybody. 'Ahem, Hello... Hey everyone!? How 'bout paying a little attention here?!' I went as far as just the other side of the single-strand wire fence. I knew I couldn't lead him right to them -- they'd bolt. I had to let nature take its course.

At this point, I was Praying with a capital P, that nature would please take the lead. It did. Or someone did. 'Hello again God. It's me again, the one with the fawn. Whatever you did and however you did it, you got me through a goodbye, and the little fawn heading into freedom and his future. Thanks.' I couldn't have done it on my own, that I knew.

Baby Buck did see the other deer, and went trotting over to them. He wasn't exactly welcomed, but they didn't chase him off either. So he hung around, sort of watching them, but also doing some exploring on his own, taking in the surroundings. Then I noticed he began to do what they were doing, browsing for forage. Aha! He was on his way to becoming a deer in the wild. This was wonderful to see, a great lift for me emotionally, and went a long way toward helping me accept his leaving.

Very slowly and little by little, I withdrew until I was sitting on the stoop of my mini deck in the back yard, and stayed there for I don't remember how long. Two or three times Baby Buck came to me. I patted him, and talked to him, and then, reinforced --apparently he'd just needed a 'mama-fix' -- he would return to the group of deer. So far so good.

Then came a considerably long stretch of time when he didn't come to me. That brought on a real mixed bag of feelings simultaneously -- I was glad for him and sad for me, but overall, more glad for him. It seemed like a good time to go about my daily routine with my dogs and horses. I kept looking over into the field of course, eyeing his activity and progress in making friends with the does. Then the does headed back toward the woods, with Baby Buck tagging along! Good for YOU! I thought, and promptly burst into tears.

Soon though, being with my dogs and horses dispelled my sadness. It wasn't that I didn't spend the next 4 ½ hours thinking about Baby Buck, wondering where he was, how and what he was doing, if he was still with the does, and if he'd be in for his 10 pm bottle, because I did. Being one who always has fun with my dogs and horses though, because they're fun and sweet, interactions with them helped raise my spirits.

Dusk came about 9 pm, and I returned to the back yard stoop, with a cup of tea, you know, just hanging out, savoring the last vestiges of a pretty summer day, listening to the night sounds of the pastoral setting, yada yada yada. Right. We all know what I was really doing. At dark, I turned on a few house lights, the floodlights outside the house, the barn lights and outside spots, the star's timer had already clicked on, and waited for you-know-who.

Just before 10 pm I warmed a bottle, and put some carrots and grain in a bowl. Would he appear? 10 pm came and went. I remember the sinking feeling in my heart, though it was followed by pep-talk bravado and upbeat thoughts like, this meant good things for him, that he was doing ok, was maybe still with the does, bedding down near them now, feeling confident enough to stay out on his own in the night, without a 'mama fix'. That was good for him I knew, and I made myself be happy for him. Soon I felt genuinely happy for him.

About 10:30 I was just getting up to go inside, teasing myself with 'well, maybe he'll come in tomorrow…', when out of the corner of my eye I saw a silhouette approaching. 'Baby Buck has arrived again!' I was one happy camper! And he seemed glad to see me. He sort of nuzzled with me for a few moments, then stood quietly while I patted and talked to him, seeming in no rush for his bottle or bowl, as if it really was me he was glad to see, not just his food.

And of course, that's exactly how it was -- because to him, I was his mama. Though keep remembering, I still didn't know how cemented our bond was and would be for the next four years. I don't even remember the exact point at which it finally dawned on me that this fellow's not leaving, ever, and that Baby Buck is mine and I'm his, for the duration. At some point I know it must have. But that night, the feeling that he was genuinely glad to see me, not just for his treats, did my heart a gazillion goods. He had his bottle, veggies and grain, hung around for a bit, then headed back into the field and was gone into the night. I did leave the lights in the barn on just in case he came back sometime through the night. Actually I did that for a few nights running just after his release. After he'd left, I let the dogs out, hayed the horses and headed to bed.

Chapter 7

Like a kid at Christmas I couldn't WAIT to get up the next morning and see what might be under the tree…or in the yard…or in the barn? I'd left the light on in 'his' stall, the stall and barn doors open, and the horses blocked out of the run-in shed, in case he came in overnight. Though it was still dark, I fixed the dogs their breakfast, let them out and played with them a bit. I know it seemed early to them, only because it was, but they never turned down food or play no matter the hour. I grained and hayed the horses, then turned them out to pasture.

Then, my vigil began. Daybreak came. Daybreak went. I began weeding to get a head start on the heat, as the day promised to be a real scorcher, and other than mad dogs and Englishmen…well, we all know what they say about them. Something poked my shoulder as I knelt over the dahlias -- Baby Buck! I jumped and he jumped because I jumped, and then I dropped down and gave him a big hug and nuzzle. Gosh was it good to see him. He looked great, not a scratch on him. His first night on his own obviously had gone well. 'Hello God, s'me again. Thanks, for, well, you know… .'

I went in and got his bottle and bowl. He was waiting in the same spot where I left him. He didn't follow me up on to the deck, which I took as a good thing, as I've got lots of sliding glass doors which could cause trouble, as they sometimes do with birds who try to fly through them. I think he had caught on to when 'mama' goes to that 'place', she'll be right back, and with food! Smart boy, I *was* right back and with food.

Throughout his fawn-hood, there were certainly lots of times that Baby Buck trotted or ran in, occasionally throwing in a leap or two here and there for good measure. But there were times when still a fawn, that he ambled in, and ambled out. It seemed to fit his nature, of which I spoke earlier -- calm, cool and collected. As he neared yearling age, he was a total 'ambler'. When a full-grown mature buck, with antlers, his amble took on a slow and stately pace, majestic almost. Never once in the time I knew him, did I ever see him riled, antsy, hurried, or flustered.

I mention this now, because during the first days following his release, I didn't know quite what to make of what I was seeing when he came in. Sometimes he would come in running as if something was chasing him or he was super hungry, and other times, even with my calling, he would do this ambling thing. I thought maybe he wasn't feeling well, or was sore for some reason. It took me some time to appreciate that this was just his demeanor and carriage maturing as he did.

Those first days and weeks following his release, and actually through the Fall, actually for the next four years, I could have pretty much set my watch by his comings. They began at the crack of dawn, and continued throughout the day just about every four hours. There was evidently no mama who'd adopted him to the point of letting him nurse from her, as he took a bottle from me four times a day.

From about late August on, I began weaning him, decreasing the amounts of milk little by little, coinciding with upping the amount of veggies and grain. It was late October when I removed the milk altogether. He had grown a lot, as you'll see from his photos, was in excellent shape body fat and bulk-wise, and was obviously finding plenty of forage on his own in the woods.

His very first days after release were spent exploring every inch of my yards, flower beds and banks, the front fenced-in field along my driveway, and the dog pen. He would lie right outside the dog pen, and rest, sometimes when one or two of my dogs were inside the pen. Neither the dogs nor Baby Buck seemed overly interested in one another, and everybody seemed to adopt a 'live and let live' attitude. That certainly seemed a plus.

The following Spring however, things changed -- not in a bad way -- but as the dogs ran around in the pen, Baby Buck would run the fence line with them. Everyone got exercise, and I think they all thought it was a fun game. I think the only thing my dogs may have wondered was 'how come the big guy doesn't have to be in the fence too?'

He tried to come up on my deck, [and that one time had made it when he thought he and the puppies were playing 'tag'], so I blocked it off with chairs because it didn't seem like a good idea to have him up there. That changed later -- his idea not mine.

I kept his grain in a can on the deck which was easier than going to the barn for it every time. I think I began this with Lone Fawn. When he'd come in, I'd fix his bowl and meet him in the yard, or at the barn or wherever he was, and give it to him there. That following Spring, I was upstairs in my bedroom and thought I heard someone on the deck. I went out onto the deck off my bedroom, to see who had come to visit.

As I called "yoo-hoo…?", looking down toward the corner of the house which cantilevers near the front door, [and it's in this cantilevered spot that the can of grain was kept], Baby Buck peeked around that same corner and was looking up at me from the deck. What a sight.

My camera though was nowhere near, but the image is clear as a bell. Though I tried to sound stern in asking him just what he was doing, I had to laugh. I went downstairs, and very slowly out to where he was on the deck. As usual, he was calm as could be, just waiting for his grain. So I obliged, and from then on, more often than not, he ate on the deck.

Fortunately, he never got confused by the sliding glass doors. Or who knows, maybe sometime when I wasn't there, he had 'met' one of them and learned that they were not penetrable. There were many times when I drove up the driveway and he'd be on the deck near his grain can. That first time of finding him there as I drove up, I went and stood by him while I used the remote to close the garage door, thinking its grating sounds might startle him. He heard it and listened, but hardly moved a muscle. There also was one time I found him at the grain can with the lid off, and having a wonderful 'pig-out'.

Starting later Summer, he often appeared in the company of various other deer, a doe with or without fawns, or fawns with or without a doe. Like Lone Fawn and John Doe he had reached that place of being able to walk both worlds, being with deer and being with me. And like them, he would leave the group to come for a visit or his treats, and they would watch him intently as he approached me. He'd have his bottle and/or bowl, and either hang around for awhile with me, or go back to his deer friends and browse with them.

Sometimes he would come in with other deer, and after his bowl and/or bottle, remain here the rest of the day. If the weather was 'fittin', I'd stay outside for awhile with him, doing chores, garden, or barn work. He'd just follow along with me. In seasons to come, and remember there were four-years-worth of seasons with him, when I spent a lot of time outside, working in the flower beds, or other, he would just lie down in the yard and rest, and literally just hang out with me.

Chapter 8

Back to his first Fall.

One afternoon he came in with a young doe about his size, so I guessed she might be about his age. They seemed to be good pals who traveled and spent at least a fair amount of time together. I named her "Lilly", as she was a very pretty doe, and lilies in my view are one of the prettiest of flowers. If I thought she was pretty, I felt certain she must have caught Baby Buck's eyes. But I've no idea.

She was stand-offish as far as approaching me, which was understandable. She would watch him as he came right to me and had his bowl, as I patted him, stroked his thickening coat, and as we had our nuzzles. She would look from him, to his bowl, to me, and back again to him. Her curiosity was growing. A couple of times she began to approach as he ate from the bowl, always half-hiding behind him. As usual, I always talked to him, and even before I named her, I'd started including her in the conversations.

One particularly nice afternoon, the two had come in at some point and were lying together in the front yard. I called a hello to them through the sliding glass door, and went out to give Baby Buck his bowl of grain and treats. This time, I grabbed an extra bowl and treats. As soon as I got outside, they were both up, and he was waiting just off the deck, she behind him in hide-mode. I put down his bowl, then a few feet away I put the second bowl for her. I backed up a bit and sat on the deck step.

Inch by excruciating inch she began tip-toeing nearer, hiding behind him until finally she emerged from behind and took her first bite from the bowl. I think she was thrilled, not only with the grain, but also with the carrots, and she ate every morsel. With Winter not far off, she too would need all the extra sustenance and nutrition she could get, so I was happy to feed her too. And I was extra happy that 'my boy' seemed to have a special friend. Whether they might become more than friends later, when both reached maturity, I had no way of divining.

It did get me wondering whether I could risk not neutering him until later, after the next Fall, thinking not only how fun it would be for me to get to see an offspring of Baby Buck's, because I felt certain he would bring his fawn around for me to see, but also knowing his exceptionally calm nature and temperament would be carried on into future generations of deer. That would be a good thing I thought, and he would have a legacy. There was still ample time to think about all that and decide. It was such fun to imagine a baby-Baby Buck, [wait, I'd had one of those already!], or Baby Buck the Second? BB II? Junior? Or…Babette? Well…I'd hope for a boy.

That Fall, the scene of Baby Buck and Lilly lying in my front yard, and then having a meal from their bowls, repeated itself over and over. Though by no means tame, little by little, Lilly became less wary of me, and came to her bowl more and more readily. I know that I took photos of the two of them, but from inside the house because I was pretty sure that camera would scare off Lilly. I have looked everywhere with no luck. Where I did find them was on my videos, hardly useful here. Now maybe….. if they make this into a movie…. no, that's never going to fly… who would they get to play Baby Buck? Robin Williams can play just about any role, but even he couldn't pull off this one.

It was also that Fall that Baby Buck met my Golden Retriever Sadie face-to-face, by total accident. They had seen one another before, but separated by the wire fence of the dog pen. He was having a bottle just off my back deck. Suddenly, there was Sadie right next to us, and him, sniffing him all over. I'd obviously not shut the front door tightly, and typical Golden, she had to meet and investigate every visitor. She was six years old by then, so fairly settled as Goldens go, and knowing their gentle temperaments, I knew she was no threat to him. I was also pretty sure he was no threat to her. He did stop chugging long enough to exchange a few sniffs with her, then went back to his bottle. She sat down next to me and just watched.

When he finished, they had some more sniffing interactions with both tails wagging and bodies wriggling -- well, Sadie was doing most of the wriggling, another typical Golden habit. I stayed on the alert, ready to play referee in case it was needed, but it wasn't. They each milled around the back yard for a few minutes, near but not paying attention to one another. Sadie came and lay down next to me. Baby Buck came over to me [and Sadie] once before he left, for a few parting pats and snuggles, and then wandered over to the back field.

Chapter 9

So often Baby Buck spent whole days here, moving from spot to spot. I'd find him by the flower beds, the dog pen and back side of the house where in summer it is wonderfully cool, shaded by a big Bradford pear tree. Or he would lie in the pastures. Sometimes he could be seen browsing right alongside my horses. Of all these places, the front yard under the maple near the flower beds was his favorite spot.

As I mentioned way back, neither he nor any fawn I raised ever ate any of my flowers. I think that's pretty remarkable and I certainly appreciated it. I think he liked the front yard best because it's sloped and broad, and therefore offers a panoramic view -- of the front field, my driveway and the paths beside it where the deer often walked, the woods just off the driveway, the barn and pasture below it, and the woods just below it. Sitting on its little knoll he could survey the whole scene, looking over his kingdom as it were. I'd often go sit next to him, with a good book. He'd chew his cud and I'd read. Sweet times those were.

My favorite place to find him at night, was lying along the dog pen where it met the back side of the house, because it was just below my bedroom window. The first night I saw him there, I couldn't quite believe it, and thought it must be total coincidence. After all it was a spot he frequented during the day, especially summer days when it was hot. But I'd never noticed him staying that close by the house at night, I hadn't called him to that spot at night, and it wasn't just summer when he slept there. There were so many nights when I'd be going to bed and look down to see him lying there, and I'm speaking of many nights over a 4-year period, that I became less and less sure that it was coincidence. I'd tell him good night, and whatever else, and he'd look up as if to say the same. He'd still be there in the morning.

It was certainly unusual to have a deer sleep outside my bedroom window, but considering who it was, and our 'history', it certainly seemed plausible that it was one more reflection of our connection and his continuing perception of me simply as 'mama'. Or it could be simply that after the first time I saw him there and spoke to him, this in itself reinforced his returning there for so many nights. Whatever it was, there was something comforting and protective about his being there. I wondered if he felt somewhat the same.

No matter what time of year, Baby Buck was in early every morning, and at least twice a day. There were days he was here three and four times, and days he stayed all day. He also frequently went into the barn, sometimes to just look around, sometimes to rest. And often, when it was pouring or storming, or cold and snowing, I'd see him go in through the run-in shed into his old stall. I honestly don't know if he ever did that when one of the horses was already in there, but if so, they apparently worked out an arrangement, as I never saw him, or a horse, bolt out of the stall, I never heard any commotion, and I never saw any 'war wounds' on anybody.

Many a winter night when he'd come in for his last feed of the day, he followed me right into the barn without hesitation. Some of those nights, he'd already be in the barn waiting for me to appear with his food. I have lots of video of him coming into the barn on cold snowy nights, and of him peeking out waiting for me to arrive.

We took many walks together in the woods. The horse and deer trails made it easy to travel to lots of different spots, and along the way we'd see all sorts of other critters- deer, groundhogs, opossum, squirrels, rabbits and turkeys. There were wonderful overgrown nooks we used to stop in for a little rest, or to watch the animals' activities. It was Baby Buck who usually picked out these spots. He'd fold up quick-as-you-please, [boy did THAT bring back memories and I'd tell him, "like you couldn't just *do* that when I tried to give you that first bottle?!"], plop down and look at me as if to say, 'well, c'mon...you can get under here too'. And under I'd crawl.

By the Fall of '94 he had not developed antlers, unless I'm totally mistaken and have forgotten. From the few photos of him that November, [mostly Polaroids], like the one below, I can't see any signs of them.

I think this is why I felt fairly certain that he'd be pretty safe during his first hunting season. Also I had contacted those few fellows who hunted the property adjacent to our neighborhood, and neighbors on adjacent hills, the ones I'd spoken to about John Doe, now to tell them about Baby Buck. I think I even showed them the photos. And they all said they would be on the lookout for him.

It was the hunters who reminded me that his not being even a yearling, but just that year's fawn whose small size would point him out as such, would be a built-in added protection. Another reason I felt assured was the fact that he spent so much time here, where he was safe.

So while I know there were surely days when I had anxious moments during his first hunting season, there weren't many of them because he seemed to always be right here. If he wasn't visible, as soon as I'd call him, it would be mere seconds before he'd appear, so he was obviously staying close. It would be the following year's hunting season when my worries would increase -- he would be older than a yearling, and most likely, he would have antlers.

Antlers are fascinating, the status symbols of male supremacy among the deer. They're used to attract prospective mates, and to intimidate rival males. Deer antlers are supposedly the fastest growing things in the animal kingdom. In Summer the antlers are encased in velvet, which is nutrient-supplying and filled with blood. As Fall and breeding season approach, bucks rub off the velvet using the bark of trees. Then they polish their antlers, again using tree bark but also anything else that's handy like fence posts, and voila, they really are the handsome studs they think they are!

My boy did begin to grow his in the Spring of '95, qualifying him as a "button buck". I used to jokingly call him "Baby Button-Buck". He didn't get it I know, but it always gave me a little chuckle. The pedicles, or buttons, which become the base for the full set of antlers, had sprouted around May 9. Remember, I had no camera in '95 which means no photos. They grew fast and by mid-May were 2 ½ inches long.

I can't explain why, during all the time that had elapsed since his release, I hadn't gotten him neutered. Although, knowing that the real physical danger to me would not manifest until he reached the age of two or so, [he was just one year then], probably gave me a sense of safety personally.

Add to that, I'd never seen the slightest hint of aggressiveness, or ill-humor toward me, and we'd been spending a great deal of time together. I mentioned earlier that I had at one time thought about not neutering him until after he'd had a chance to perhaps breed, so that may have played into my thinking. But that meant he would have to get through a hunting season with antlers, and possibly with what a hunter would deem a prize rack. It also meant that he'd be closer to two years old, and therefore closer to the aggressiveness I'd been warned about. The thought that he'd get antlers that might be prized by some hunter was reason enough to neuter him and thereby potentially prevent any future antler development or growth. And of course, the side perk of not being mauled to death by him was definitely a selling point.

I talked with the deer expert at the university in early May, when Baby Buck's pedicles appeared. He was practically a yearling, which was late to neuter, as far as preventing antler growth altogether. According to the expert, to absolutely stop antler development or growth, neutering had to be done by 20 weeks of age, or 5 months. He may have told me this in connection with John Doe, but the notation about it was in Baby Buck's notes.

Regardless, we were where we were as far as Baby Buck's age. He did tell me that if he any antlers did develop post-neuter, they would always stay in velvet, and that antlers in velvet are no prize to hunters. That was grand news. I would have to bank on that as a protection from hunters. Also, if he got antlers, he would lose them in winter just like the regular bucks do.

In that conversation, he went over with me what sedatives to use, the dosage for his weight of approximately one hundred pounds, the supplies I'd need, and the many miscellaneous things I'd need to do before, during and after the neutering. As I said I would in the neutering part of John Doe's story, I now refer you back to that section if you want to refresh your memory about the procedures and details.

Chapter 10

I talked to my Vet, and we made general plans for his neutering. I got the sedative from him, and got all my supplies together. The third week of May our weather was exceptionally temperate, low humidity, comfortable temperatures, and no precipitation. We chose May 24. I don't remember being as concerned about Baby Buck's neutering process as about John Doe's, mostly because Baby Buck was proving to be so predictable in his comings and goings. He was in early every morning, without fail, rain or shine.

The one tricky unknown might be getting the injection of the sedative into him, as I'd never had to give him any shots. It would be something totally new to him. So about five days before D-Day, or N-Day, I began desensitizing him with my fingernails to pokes, pricks and pinches on the back side of both thighs. I did it while he was eating from his bowl, as that's when I would have to do it the morning of his neutering, and there was no reaction from him at all, no flinch, no head turn, no nothing. That was a good sign, and gave me extra confidence that things would go well.

The only other unknown was how long it would take the sedative to take effect, [the span being 7 to 12 minutes for any of you who didn't go back and refresh your memories], and how far he might wander before the sedative took full effect. Those answers could only be known after the shot had been given. I would hope and pray that the answers to both would be minimal.

Actually there was another Pre-Op concern. It had to do with the part where just as he began to drop from the effect of the sedative, I had to get the tarp and blankets directly under him and at the same time make sure he didn't drop too hard. The concern was that this would be with a one hundred-pound deer, significantly larger than the seventy pounds John Doe had been. So it was another unknown as to how I'd manage this, the split-second timing of getting my hands out from under his one hundred pounds just before he dropped, [and crushed them], and being able to help his one hundred-pound frame down without him hitting too hard. Time and that morning would tell.

May 25 dawned sunny and dry. I had fed the horses and the dogs while it was still dark, and was waiting just outside the barn for Baby Buck, with his bowl, a few treats, and the shot. It was 6 am. At 6:05 he arrived, and followed me into the barn. As he took his first bites, I gave him the shot in the back right thigh. He didn't flinch. I called the Vet to tell him I'd just given the shot. He took a few more bites, stopped eating, turned around facing me, and stood just staring at me. The drug was already beginning to take effect. It seemed to be working fast, or at least a lot faster than with John Doe. I've always wondered if it began acting so quickly in part due to his calm nature.

Then he walked out of the barn, along the back side of the house past the dog pen, across the front yard, each step less steady than the one before. I hoped he might drop in the front yard, but before he reached the slope. He didn't, but kept going, across and down the slope of the front yard where he almost fell. I was beginning to get nervous, and knew that even if I wanted to stop him from wandering any farther, I doubted I'd be physically able to do that, especially if his plan was to keep going. And that apparently was his plan, or where his mind and body were taking him under the influence of the drug.

Thankfully he made it down the front yard slope without crashing, across the driveway, to the brush just beyond it which is at the edge of the woods. It was there, about fifteen feet from the drive, that he dropped. I was able get the tarp and blankets under his body just before he went down, and my hands out of the way before he fell on them, but I wasn't strong enough to help him drop slowly and gently. He landed hard and bit his tongue as he landed, which brought a little bit of blood. The sight of that scared me, but it stopped almost right away. I felt terribly that I hadn't been able to help him land softer.

His breathing seemed rapid and a bit labored, his tongue was hanging out and his mouth looked very dry. I put a towel over just his eyes, not wanting to cover his mouth or nose and possibly compromise his breathing further. I lifted his head and neck onto my lap which would aid his breathing. By this time, it was about 6:15 and I was really anxious for the Vet to arrive, which didn't happen until 6:45. I remember it as if it was yesterday -- it was the longest thirty minutes I'd ever spent.

What a huge relief when I heard his truck coming up the drive. Despite the outward signs that had me worried, the Vet assured me that his heart and lungs sounded excellent, his pulse was good, and that the rapid somewhat labored breathing was often typical for sedated ruminants. He examined his tongue, said he'd just nicked it and it would be fine.

At 6:50 he gave him the anesthetic, and we waited while it took effect, which was only about three or four minutes. Once again he checked his vitals, which were still fine, and then he performed the neutering procedure. That took about five minutes. Over the next hour, the Vet checked his vitals four times, and each time they were fine. At 8:15 he checked them once more, pronounced them normal, and left.

Remembering that John Doe had been out for a good four hours, I settled back for what I thought would be a long stretch. Surprise-surprise - - just 1 ¾ hours later, at 10 am, Baby Buck woke up, got up, took a few very groggy steps then lay right back down. He did that once more about fifteen minutes later, a little more alert. Each time I did manage to grab the tarp and blankets and get them underneath him. At one point he began to shiver. It was warm out, though breezy, and I worried the breeze had given him a chill. I called the Vet, who reassured me that the shivering was normal after an anesthetic, an involuntary response and not any sign that he'd caught a chill.

From about 10:30 until 1:15 pm he rested comfortably, napping on and off. By 1:30 his breathing was completely back to normal, the shivers were gone, and he seemed very alert. He got up and walked with a steady gait over to the bird bath in the front yard, took a few sips, then continued into just the edge of the woods below the barn, where he lay down, closed his eyes and fell asleep. Talk about coincidence -- this was the same spot John Doe had chosen to rest after his neutering.

Throughout the rest of the day, I monitored him from my windows, and whenever his eyes were open, I went over to check on him more closely. The drugs were obviously still working their way out of his system, but by later afternoon, his eyes lost that glazed look and were clear again. I felt we were basically out of the woods. I stayed sitting with him, from 4:30 until about 6:30, when he got up. That time, he seemed totally steady on his feet. He milled about in the pasture, then headed off into the woods behind the barn.

He came back in around 9 that evening, and though I could offer him only a few bites of food, not the full amount until the next morning, he stayed for about an hour, resting in the front yard, wanting to be patted. He got up and headed to the back side of the house. I thought I knew where he was going.

There were a few housekeeping things I had to do in the kitchen. After about a half hour, I went upstairs to my bedroom and couldn't help but look out and down. There he was, keeping his vigil, or whatever it was below my bedroom window. I would never know exactly. All I knew was that that night, I was particularly grateful to have him close by. 'Hello, God? It's me, and gosh have we had a day…but then, you know that…Thanks for bringing Baby Buck through things all right…for steadying me…and especially for having him under the window tonight where I can keep an eye on him.'

Making comparisons later with John Doe's neutering only ended up confusing me. The sedative had taken only five minutes to take effect with Baby Buck, [so much for that 7-minute minimum]; it took twice that long for John Doe to drop, and he was 30 pounds smaller.

Granted, the dose was smaller than Baby Buck's, but dosages are in proportion to weight. Maybe that old adage "the bigger they are, the harder they fall" is true after all. Overall, Baby Buck's neutering did not go as smoothly, perhaps mostly, or even totally attributable to his greater weight.

The next morning I overslept my usual early morning rising, and when I looked out, Baby Buck was not in his spot below the window. It was going on 9 am, so I really wasn't surprised that he'd gotten a start on his day. There was a group of deer in the back field, and though visibility was limited by a haze, I thought I could see him among them. If it was, he didn't come over, and therefore I thought he wasn't particularly hungry or maybe was a little leery of me after his experiences the previous day. I went about my day, but always keeping my eyes open for him, with his bowl of food and treats at the ready.

By 6:30 that evening I still hadn't seen him, for sure anyway, and I was worried. I'd taken his bowl with me when I went to put out hay for the horses and was heading back toward the house when I noticed a lone deer standing on the path beyond the barn. I called 'Baby Buck' a few times. This lone deer looked up and stayed where it was. My heart sank. I tried one more call, and this deer looked up again, and then started trotting in my direction -- it was him!, and one of the few times since fawn hood that he'd come in trotting. I had my video camera with me, and caught it on tape. Once again I have a special moment on video only, but I'm grateful to have images no matter what the format.

This was the first time I'd seen him since the night before, and as he trotted in, his gait was normal with no signs that he was sore from the neutering. He came into the barn with no hesitation, and greeted me with a few nuzzles. If he'd had any bad memory-association with the barn, since he'd gotten his shot in there, or with me since I was the one who'd given him the shot, both were gone, and it was like old times. He was interested first in sharing some nuzzle-time. Then he went to his bowl, and ate every bit of food in his bowl. I tagged along with him when he left the barn.

He stopped at the feeder that the Porters had given me for John Doe. He took a few bites of grain from it, then wandered into the front field below the front yard where he lay down for awhile. Several deer went through the field, with Lilly among them. She saw him, walked to him and folded herself up right next to him. It was a cozy scene.

Chapter 11

I've not spoken yet about the fact that deer do not all look alike, other than sharing the same basic shape and form. So when I say above that I saw Lilly among the group, it was through recognizing her face and particular features, that I knew it was she. When I mention any of the fawns I raised, and being able to pick them out even at far distances, it is because each deer's face, ear set, body configuration and confirmation, bone structure and gait is different and unique to it. As with humans, between mamas and their fawns there are strong often identical genetic similarities, including face shapes and coloring for instance, so that one can tell immediately whose fawn is whose, based on the mama's physical and physiological characteristics.

Also, the coloring on deer faces is not mono-tone, but two-or even three-tone. Whatever combination this pattern of tones takes on mama's face, the fawn's facial attributes will be practically an exact replica. It's fascinating really. The next time the opportunity presents itself to view some deer, really look at them, their faces especially and you'll see how different each looks. It's something I'd never have known if it hadn't been for the fawns I raised.

Over the years, I've often played a sort of game about this, and quizzed myself on who's who among the regulars that come here. It's especially challenging to try it at different times of the year, and particularly with the bucks, with and without antlers. I have to take pictures of them so I have some means of checking my answers. On the whole I do fairly well, but then many of the regulars have been coming here for five or more years.

In neutering Baby Buck, we accomplished two crucial things: if he developed antlers, they would always stay in velvet, affording him protection from hunters; and, the aggressiveness which he would develop somewhere around two to three years old, and which would be directed at me, had been eliminated. This last, the expert at the university said he could guarantee one hundred per cent.

As I mentioned, I have no photos of him from '95. His neutering had stopped his antler growth completely, at least for then, so as hunting season began, the worries I thought I would have because he would most likely have antlers, were much less than I had anticipated. That and the fact that he was here ninety-five per cent of the time made for many fewer anxious moments.

I have to confess to still calling him in during hunting season, and I did this every hunting season, sometimes several times a day and especially on days that seemed made for a hunter weather-wise, cold, clear, and a bit of snow on the ground enabling better tracking. At last December 31 arrived. He'd made it through his second hunting season.

He was becoming a large fellow -- bulky, muscular, and fit, with evident and ample stores of body fat. In fact, there were a few times over the years when he got a little 'portly'. But to me, he was always the most handsome buck of any that passed through, even the 'Big Boys' with their showy racks. And this applied to early Springs when his antlers had just begun to grow, or later in the years once they were fully grown and velveted.

It was fascinating to watch him walk among the other bucks. It definitely seemed as if they'd all met before and were friends even. At least they got along ok. He would stroll through them, interact or not with one or more of them, or they with him, and keep ambling with that stately poise, as if he were on his way to a cabinet meeting or something. I know - - that *is* anthropomorphism.

But he just had an air about him, that the other bucks apparently liked well enough, and respected. It seemed more than just toleration, as never once did I see any of them challenge him, or be irritable or threatening toward him, and more often than not, it was the other bucks who initiated friendly interactions.

Perhaps his calm self-assured demeanor, and lack of 'wired' behavior during breeding time, had a sedating effect on them, who knows. What I do know is what I observed -- the big boys could be running around as they do during breeding season, acting panicky, erratically leaping here and there especially when does would appear on the scene, and if Baby Buck arrived, or hung around nearby, they calmed down, and became quiet and still. It was extraordinary to watch. When he'd leave, or come over to me, their frantic activities would begin anew. In the following photo taken November '96, Baby Buck is in the left foreground, and one of the 'Big Boys' is in the right background.

The photo below is of a few of Baby Buck's 'Big Boy' friends.

Winter wore on, and soon it was Spring 1996. I have always loved this time of year when the deer shed their dull gray-brown coats of Fall and Winter, and come Spring, the sleeker coats with their rich and lush deep sorrel colors replace the grays and browns. It's actually possible to see the transitions from one coat to the other on a deer. On some it's more pronounced and noticeable than on others. Part of their coat will have begun to turn into Spring colors, while the other is still in the Winter colors. It's not a look that Versacce or Chanel would ever have gone for, but it's unique.

That Spring, Baby Buck's coat transformed into a beauty – of course, I may be a bit prejudiced.

As you can see, his antlers had begun growing again. It happened right around the time of his 2nd birthday which was May 14 or so. Over the summer months I was in an almost constant state of curiosity to see how they would develop beyond the beginning pedicles. In the back of my mind, I was still banking on their staying in velvet as a safeguard against hunters. Stay in velvet they did, and every subsequent year, for which I was very grateful.

Those summer days were pretty much repeats of the previous ones of any season. As I've said, it would be too repetitive for readers, but to me, it was never dull, or boring, or 'ho-hum-another-day-with-Baby Buck.' The uniqueness of having a basically pet deer never got old. On the contrary, as days and years progressed, he endeared himself to me more and more.

Chapter 12

That July he had a very special visitor, one of my all-time favorite people, "Little Moo", also know by other family members as "Aunt Moo", or just "Moo", or "Muriel", or, as my Father called her, "Duchess". She is not a relative of my side of the family at all, but is what genealogists refer to as "fictive kin" -- someone who becomes so closely affiliated with a family, and becomes so like family, that over time, they're called cousin, or aunt or uncle. She's the type of person everyone wants in their family because she's so fun, effusive and dynamic.

Little Moo, her husband, and one of her four sons were here visiting some of their real relatives, [they live in New England], and at a family gathering, I told her about Baby Buck. Being a big animal-person herself, she couldn't wait to meet him, and came mid-afternoon the next day. I made us some iced teas, and we sat on the deck steps that lead into the front yard to await his arrival. I had his bowl, and called him.

I might just as well have said "cue the deer", because in no more than ten seconds, Baby Buck came around the corner of the screened porch and ambled on over to us. That brought a burst of laughter from her, and she wanted to know if someone hiding around the corner held him until I called. I told her he was tame, but not that tame.

He came to me first, for some nuzzles and pats, and then moved over to Little Moo and let her pat him. She was totally charmed, awed, and, she said, "instantly in love with this magnificent gentle creature." She couldn't get over how calm and gentle he was, and wanted to hear all about him, every detail. That's the sort of person she is, no perfunctory "how are you?", she wants to hear it all, because she's genuinely interested.

I gave her the condensed version of his story up to that point, showed her a few of his fawn pictures, [typical mama eh? pulling out the baby pictures…], told her about his neutering, [and that thanks to it we were able to sit here nuzzling with him rather than fleeing for our lives], his friend Lilly, and how he'd been here every day since his release two years ago. That absolutely floored her.

After his greetings to us, he ate the grain from his bowl, which at first I held, then passed to Little Moo to hold. I always wished I'd taken photos of her visit, because throughout it she was as wide-eyed and grinning as those little 3 and 4 year olds had been in my barn. He finished his grain and treats, and remained standing right in front of us. She leaned forward to pat and nuzzle him, and he returned the nuzzles, which elated her. He had her in the palm of his… hoof -- just where he'd had me for the last two years.

After a few more nuzzles with each of us, he went and lay down in his favorite spot in the front yard, only ten feet from us, with the branch of the maple shading him, relaxing and chewing his cud. Little Moo and I continued visiting for another half hour or so, and then she had to leave, though she kept repeating that she really didn't want to go. And I knew she meant it. What was extra nice was that she appreciated him so much, and recognized how very special he was. She kept referring to him as enchanting. That's a word I've not yet used in his descriptions, but it certainly fits. When she said it I thought, she really has him pegged. She said goodbye to him, and then we had our goodbye and she left. I went and sat with Baby Buck. I passed along all the nice things she'd said about him, and told him how right she was. We stayed there under the shade of the maple for another hour or so. Then I had things to do, and so did he apparently, as he headed off to the back field where some deer were browsing.

As the Summer months of 1996 continued, Baby Buck's antlers kept growing in their velvet wrapping. One thing I haven't said is how much he loved having his ears stroked, starting as a fawn and that very first time we had together the day he arrived. One thing he did not like, and I think it was the only thing, or the only thing I ever discovered, was having his antlers touched. I don't know why that would be, except that maybe the velvet casing is particularly sensitive to touch. Once when I was stroking his ears, I accidentally touched one of his antlers, and when I did, he quickly ducked, pulled his head away and shook it back and forth a few times. I got the message and made certain I never touched them again.

Chapter 13

Soon it was September, then October -- hunting season. With his antlers in velvet, and his being here on my property or just off it ninety-nine per cent of the time, I felt that he was fairly safe. The signs from our days of posting when John Doe was here, were still up and visible. Not that I checked them all, but in the course of walks and riding my horses, I saw that there were still plenty.

Then a sort of wild idea came to me, and I called the fellows who hunted the property adjacent to our neighborhood, the ones I'd called about John Doe. After a very brief overview, I invited them to "Tea with Baby Buck". My plan was to show them Baby Buck 'in person', and if he didn't come in I could show them photos.

My pitch would be to ask them to please watch for him, and obviously, not to shoot him. The one unknown would be that he didn't necessarily always come in late afternoons, and that was the earliest these fellows could come as they all worked. So I might have to rely on the photos. I forged ahead, made cookies, and had beer and tea on hand. My money was on the beer, though I felt I should have tea available, since it was part of the invitation.

So October 24 1996, at about 5:15 pm, my invitees arrived, all three of them and a friend who sometimes hunted with them. Then, and over the years, I could just imagine their 'locker-room' talk or what they told their wives about the 'crazy lady who had the deer a few years ago and called us to say please don't shoot him….well, now she has another one and invited us to come have TEA with him!' Even I had to admit it sounded a bit bizarre, but if it safeguarded Baby Buck, I didn't mind at all how I was seen, bizarre or anything else.

I set up a little buffet on the dining room table, which looks out on the front yard and deck steps. It was nice to meet the fellows face-to-face. They were as congenial in person as they'd been on the phone about John Doe. They even asked about him, and told me of times they had seen him, how well he had looked and how easy to spot he was with that bright yellow tag.

Then they wanted to know about the fellow they were there to meet, so I filled them in on his story, and explained that I'd go outside in a minute to get his bowl and hopefully he'd be in. We chatted a few more minutes while they enjoyed the buffet. [Beer *was* the big seller.] I went outside, got the bowl, and called Baby Buck. Then I sat down on the step and waited. Once again it was as if someone said "cue the deer", as in about ten seconds he appeared. He walked right to his bowl and began to eat. I patted him while he ate, and he gave me a couple nuzzles.

After a few more minutes, I went inside to talk with the fellows, see if they had any questions, and ask if they thought they'd be able to recognize him in the woods. What I was met with is as poignant today as it was then. All four of these big strong outdoorsy-type fellows, these bold hunters, had tears in their eyes. It was quite a moment. A couple of them tried to hide their moist eyes, turning to look back out the sliding glass door, but a couple of them unabashedly wiped their eyes while saying that they could certainly never shoot such a deer, and vowed to always be on the alert for him and to pass the word to any buddies of theirs who hunted on other adjacent hills. I couldn't ask for more than that.

We talked about his antlers always staying in velvet, according to the expert at the deer research center, which intrigued them and was something they'd not known in connection with neutering. They said that any experienced, ethical hunter, in seeing a buck with antlers still in velvet during hunting season would know that it meant something, whether a deformity, or part of a research program, or, those with more knowledge about effects of neutering on antlers might realize it could have been hand-raised, and that because of any of those factors, they would therefore let him go safely on his way.

I asked them if they were just saying that to make me feel better, and they assured me not. Knowing how they'd watched out for John Doe, having seen the tears in their eyes over Baby Buck and heard their pledges to watch out for him and spread the word, I believed they were earnest in their words. We briefly discussed that none of this would apply to poachers, because by their very illegal presence, ethical went out the window.

They added that they would be on extra- high-alert for poachers. And I had contacted the other adjacent neighborhoods describing him with his velvet antlers, asking that they be on the lookout not only for him, but for poachers. They all remembered my calls over John Doe, and they were again very willing to help.

The fellows were still enjoying the cookies and beer, so I went back out with Baby Buck while he finished his bowl. I stole a couple of glances into the dining room, and they were all watching with big grins on their faces. Baby Buck finished his bowl, and headed to the pasture below the barn where a few deer were browsing -- or perhaps waiting for him. It was after 6 and time for the fellows to leave. They each thanked me profusely, said what a treat it had been, and reiterated their pledges to watch out for Baby Buck. It had been a fun and successful gathering so I was glad the idea had come to me. It all certainly reinforced my comfort level as far as his safety during that hunting season, and the others to come.

Chapter 14

Moving right along, hunting season came and went, and true to form, Baby Buck was here more than he was anywhere else. And even when he was somewhere else, that somewhere else was never far away, because he never took long to appear when I called. Throughout that hunting season the fellows who'd come to "Tea With Baby Buck" called me from time to time to report they'd seen him and where. As the property they hunted extended all the way to our neighborhood, when they saw him in the woods, it was usually on our end so that was reassuring to know.

As the last shots were heard December 31 1996, I was feeding him just outside the barn doors. Then dark came and with it, blessed silence, and the knowledge that it would be almost a whole year before the next danger time. He'd made it through the season safely, his third.

I always welcomed in the New Year with a little more gusto during my fawn-raising years as each made it through this or that hunting season. Not that I went out and tied one on, but rather I just celebrated with whatever fawn or adult I had at the time. I made over them a little extra, gave them a few extra treats, things like that -- things that definitely would put me in the 'bizarre' category in some folks' eyes. Oh well, if you can't make over a few pet deer, who can you make over? It always was, and still is, such a relief to me when January comes, because of my fawns foremost, but I fear for my 'regulars' as well since I'd come to know them over the years, so I let out a sigh when I see them after hunting season.

Although I try not to look too closely at the regulars as they come by those first days after the end of hunting seasons. I suppose it's denial in a way, but it's too sad to see who's missing, knowing that most likely they were taken by a hunter. Inevitably though, since I know the different groups that travel together, if someone's missing, the void is evident.

Sometimes it's just that one or two are stragglers, but more often than not, it's that they're gone. It's hardest with the bucks, the big boys as I call them, they who were so magnificent-looking all antlered-up, now taken for the very thing that added so to their beauty. What a silly thing to do, so primitive, and I'll go so far as to say tacky-to-the-max, to hang parts of animals on the wall. I'm sure my thoughts about all this don't come as any surprise to the reader. Oops, I digressed a bit again. So back to our story.

Where we were was January 1997, but that's just a jumping-off point as it were. Where we're going, is fast-forwarding through the rest of the Winter, into Spring and then Summer. [I keep my promises.] He turned three years old May 14, give or take a couple of days. His antlers were growing again. Their shape, and the number of tines, was different each year. But again, they were always in velvet. By December 27, '97 he'd lost his antlers.

The deer expert's guarantee proved true: Baby Buck never developed even a hint of aggressiveness toward me. If anything, he seemed to become more docile as time and the years passed. In between his neutering, and his reaching two and then three years of age, I never even gave a thought to or had a concern about him becoming aggressive. In large part that was probably based on his behavior toward me, which never changed from the sweet, gentle, calm, nuzzling friend I always knew him to be.

Late Summer of '97 I again made contact with the hunters who'd met him, and the neighborhoods nearby, to remind them all about him, that he was antlered in velvet as before, and ask for their help in looking out for him. All of them sounded genuinely glad to hear he was still with me, and that was nice.

As in previous years, on walks or horseback rides, I made a point to check our No Hunting signs, and kept being surprised that even storms with high winds hadn't depleted their number, or anything or anyone else for that matter. So once again, heading into hunting season, I felt I'd covered the bases. And as before, with him here so much of the time and my continuing to call him in a lot, he seemed doubly protected. I always kept extra prayers going for his continued safekeeping during hunting months, on top of ones of general Thanks for his being still here and still as wonderful.

Once again, December 31 arrived, heralding the end of another hunting season. The day was an unusually warm one, the type I'd learned hunters don't like. I welcomed it, [as I did and do all such days during hunting season], and increasingly as the day kept growing nicer and warmer the later it got. In fact, Baby Buck spent the last part of the afternoon ensconced in his favorite spot in the front yard. That was an added blessing. Around 5 pm I got his bowl. He was hungry and popped right up to dine.

Afterward, he browsed around the front yard just long enough that it was dark when I saw him head toward the pasture below the barn. Baby Buck was safe for another year. He'd made it through his fourth hunting season, and was heading into his fourth year of life. It was time to celebrate and ring in the New Year, which I did the next morning, with him.

January 1 of the New Year 1998, he came in a little later than his norm. For just a few moments anxious thoughts tried to get in, but I was determined to cut them off at the pass. Finally at 7:30 he came trotting in, which I'd not see him do in some time. Jokingly I said "wha-at?...you go to some New Year's bash after you left here last night and had a hard time getting up?" He seemed extra hungry, probably due to his being late for breakfast. Maybe he had overslept. [In case the reader's wondering if I need a reality check, I knew of *course*, that he hadn't been to any New Year's bash -- he would've invited me to join him.]

It would be difficult to describe the variations in his antlers from year to year. Each year their shape and breadth was a bit different, as was their growing pattern and speed, as was the number of points. In 1998 I don't seem to have any photographs before June. Perhaps his antlers were late getting started that year, I don't remember, but the photos below show them clearly. The first was taken in July, the second in September.

At this point, Baby Buck's story is going to be put on hold, because his story overlaps with two other fawns whom you'll meet now. Then his story will resume when it converges with one of these next fawns, and their stories become intertwined.

Part IV
Bambino – My Bravest

Chapter 1

Even though Bambino's time here overlapped with the fawn that came after him, to keep a better sense of continuity, I'm going to tell his story in its entirety, before formally introducing her, as her story became intertwined with Baby Buck's. All three overlapped in time, for a time, but I think it would get too confusing and fragmented to try to tell their stories simultaneously. At least it would for me. I'll still include here some photos of him with his brief stall-mate. You'll just have to wait until later to meet her.

I don't remember the exact circumstances that brought Bambino to me, [oh, for those memory cells now flying somewhere in the ether...], except that my notes say that Sally and I picked him up June 1, 1998. According to my notes, he'd "fallen a considerable distance from a ledge on a hill." Whoever called reported that he didn't seem any worse for wear, that I do recall. Time would tell.

I imagine I got the fawn stall ready ahead of time, with the netting up and fresh sawdust mounded into cushy bedding; and that I blocked out the horses from the run-in shed. Whether they harrumphed their way to the pasture I don't remember, but five'll get you ten that there was some eye-rolling going on and maybe a 'jeez, here we go again.' Regardless, it would be time for extra apples. I'm sure I gathered my baby supplies and took them to the stall.

What I did about milk I've no idea. Whether it was goat's milk from my old friend I've also no recollection, but obviously I got some from somewhere as he had a bottle shortly after he was settled into the stall. It wouldn't surprise me to learn that the school of thought had changed by that time and that now it was ok for fawns to have just milk, generic good-ole regular milk. In fact, something must be ringing a dim bell that that was the case or I don't think I'd mention it. Or it could be that, as with humans, by the third or fourth child, parents are known to relax the rules a bit.

He was six lbs, which put him at barely one week old more or less, and born about May 24 give or take a couple of days. So tiny to be on his own. But so was Baby Buck and he'd made it just fine. He was every bit as affectionate and as much of a nuzzler as Baby Buck had been.

Early on Sally brought her young grand-daughter to visit. It was a mutual admiration society from the start between the two, and Emily returned for several visits.

Oddly enough, from the beginning he went to the bathroom on his own. I didn't have to do the 'mama thing' once, which seemed like a bonus. And there were no struggles getting him to accept the bottle, and that was like winning the lottery. Although, I honestly felt I could have played the fold-a-fawn game a bit more efficiently, maybe. After all, I'd had several practices with Baby Buck which should have taught me *some*thing. But this little guy needed no prompting to latch on to a bottle and start drinking.

The only problem was in getting his intake to increase daily, to reach the goal of 32 oz a day. For the first 11 days the most he took at a feeding was 4 ½ oz, only 18 for the day, just over half of what he needed every day. June 13 to June 18, we got up to and held at 5 oz. It wasn't until July that we got to 7 oz, and then finally 8oz at a time- the required 32 oz daily -- which carried through August 11. So that was slow going. It just seemed that his appetite got satisfied with less. He didn't look nor was he emaciated, and he was active, so it didn't seem to be having any ill effects. And it wasn't that he wasn't growing, because he was. It was just odd.

While I didn't have to do the 'mama thing' to get him going to the bathroom, he began having some minor bowel problems in that they were a little loose. The Vet had me begin Kaopectate, which helped and he was back to normal. He was to have intermittent problems, at times severe, with this the entire time he was here, although there were periods of many days in a row without problems. I know what I feel like with an upset stomach, and I imagine it's the same cross-species. It didn't quell his spirit or spirits ever, he would have bursts of activity in his stall at times, he continued to eat, and to want to nuzzle and be patted. We just couldn't seem to get a handle on his digestive problem. At different times we tried liquid Penicillin, plus Pedialite to counteract any dehydration and yogurt to counteract the negative effects of the antibiotic. He loved his yogurt and couldn't get enough of it.

Chapter 2

I'll back up a bit here, to tell you his stall-mate arrived June 19. It's almost impossible to know whether having another fawn in the stall was stressful enough to have caused his digestive problems. Considering that they didn't manifest until June 29, a week and a half after the other fawn arrived, it doesn't seem likely. Besides, they had become instant friends, nuzzling and grooming one another, resting and sleep right next to each other, and drinking their bottles side by side. I definitely believe they were a comfort to one another.

When Bambino arrived, I began keeping a notebook for him, recording his daily intake and output. The following is the first page from his notebook.

```
Baby Bambino            Mon
            TODAY'S DATE  6.1.98
                        @ 7 lbs?

● 1½ oz @ 5pm
  3½ oz - 7pm   b.m. & tinkle
  4½ oz - 11pm  b.m & tinkle

6-2 Tues
  F  5 oz -  7 am   bm & tinkle
     5 oz - 11 am   bm & tinkle
     4½ oz - 4 pm   tinkle
     4½ oz - 11 pm  tinkle

6-3 Wed
  4½ oz - 7:15 am - bm & t
  4½ oz - 1 pm
  4½ oz - 6 pm - bm & t
  4½ oz - 10:45 pm - t

● 6-4 Thurs
  4½ oz - 6:20 am - b.m. & t.
  5 oz - 12:25 pm - nope  & 1st play
  5 oz - 5:45 pm - b.m & t.  jumps, bursts
                              of activity
  5 oz - 10:45 pm - b.m. & t.
```

When the second fawn arrived, I divided the pages between the two of them, so I could record her daily intake and output. The following is a page from his-now-their notebook, with the second fawn designated as "F".

> TODAY'S DATE _____
>
> 6·20 Saturday
> B 6 oz - 7am +. ⎫ 7 5 oz - 7am
>   6 oz - 12:15p bm +•⎬   6 oz - 12:15p t
>   6 oz - 5:15p t&bm ⎭   6 oz - 5:15pm t&bm
>   6 oz - 11pm   5+ oz - 11pm
>
> 6·21 Sunday
> B 6 oz - 7am +   ⎫ V 5½ oz - 7am +
> B 6 oz - 12:15 bm •+⎬ V 3½ oz - 12:15 bm -
> B 6 oz - 5:30p bm •+⎬ V 6 oz - 5:30p bm •+
> B 6 oz - 11:15 bm&+ ⎭ V 6 oz - 11:15 p
>
> 6·22 Monday
> B 6 oz - 7am +   ⎫ V 6 oz - 7am +& l the bm
>   6 oz - 12N t&bm   ⎬   4 oz - 12N t
>   6 oz - 5:15p t&bm ⎬   5½+ oz - 5:15p
>   6 oz - 11 p   ⎭   6 oz - 11p
>
> 6·23 Tues
> ●B 6½ oz - 7am t&bm ⎫ V 6 oz - 7am +& bm butts
>   6½ oz - 12N   ⎬   5½ oz - 12N
>   6½ oz - 5pm   ⎬   4 oz - 5pm
>   6½ oz - 11pm   ⎭   4½ oz - 11pm
>
> 6·24 Wed   V
> B 6½ oz - 6am   ⎫   5 oz - 6am
>   6½ oz - 12:00   ⎬   2 oz 12:00 really
>   6½ oz - 5:30 bm   ⎬   ~~no was 4 ~~
>   4 oz - 11pm bm&t ⎭   6 oz 5:30 bm
>   6 oz - 11pm ...

Having two fawns at the same time was a bit more work, and only slightly more complicated --at feeding time for example, making sure each got the bottle at the same time. But it was also twice the fun, for the most part, and twice as sweet to have two fawns' heads resting in my lap. I remember coming to the barn for the early morning feeding those first few days, and doing almost a double-take, or think I was seeing double. They were so close in size, and therefore age, that at times they looked like twins.

They both loved nuzzling with me, getting patted, and just sitting next to me when I'd lounge with them. The three of us would curl up and take naps together. We had a lot of those sort of times, sort of nesting together, that started when the other fawn arrived, and continued until she was released -- and continued in spite of or in between Bambino's tummy troubles. They shared the stall until August 2.

Chapter 3

The evening of July 23 he began favoring his back left leg, holding it off the ground slightly and often not putting any weight on it. The area around his knee was a little swollen. I called the Vet, who said to give him one Baby Aspirin in some Pedialite in case there was any pain and to decrease inflammation, and to keep him posted. By late evening he was limping. But again, and keep this in mind throughout his story, his spirit and nature never became daunted or sour.

The limp and favoring the one leg continued on and off for the next three days, when the Vet brought his portable x-ray machine. Bambino was still his pleasant friendly self, still interacted with his stall-mate and with me, never uttered a single bleat or got grumpy. Nothing showed up on the x-rays which was great news. The next couple of days he was walking around good as new, with no sign of the limp, and the swelling around his knee gone. That was more good news. Throughout this time, his bowels were working normally.

Good news isn't necessarily any guarantee though, especially in the medical world. Just 10 days after the x-rays, Sunday August 2, disaster struck. As was my habit, every time I approached the barn I'd begin saying "hi'" -- actually I'd start as I stepped onto the back lawn from the mini-deck which is only about seventy-five feet from the barn. I'd talk loudly enough to make certain I was heard in the barn. I didn't want to startle any fawn, or my horses if they were resting in there.

About ten feet from the barn entry, I heard a 'something' that seemed to come from inside the barn. But I couldn't tell then and time hasn't helped to clarify, what exactly I heard or its origin. I wondered if I had startled him, and whether the sound I heard was him jumping up, perhaps out of a deep sleep, and that's when it happened. The thought that I might have inadvertently and obviously unintentionally caused what happened was horrendous to me.

The Vet concluded that it had most likely happened before I got to the barn, that the sound I heard was not the event happening, but him trying to get up after it and having a hard time. The 'it' was a broken tibia of his back left leg. My regular Vet was out of town for the day, which I didn't know until afterwards. I only knew I couldn't reach him. The Vet I called was one I knew, and one with a stellar reputation as a top-notch bone doctor. Thankfully, he said he would help.

The Vet said it was a bad break, and would have bled immediately. Later that day, in trying to replay what I saw when I entered the stall, I was in such a state that I have no idea whether I saw blood coming from his leg or not. I do know he wasn't making a sound, no bleating, he was just trying to stabilize himself and get ready to have his bottle. Over the years I've tried hard to recall, naturally hoping I hadn't seen any blood, which meant that he had broken it sometime earlier in the day, and that I had not been the cause. Considering events that were yet to come and the probable diagnoses, it is likely that I had not caused the broken leg. But that quasi-knowledge wouldn't sink in until some time after the fact.

The break was in the leg he had been favoring, the one with the swollen knee, the one he was limping on, for those few days-the leg that was x-rayed. The Vet suspected he had brittle bones, for whatever reason- genetic, lack of nutrition from mama for an unknown length of time, or due to the "considerable distance" he'd fallen the day he was found. Or he said it could be some combination of all of those.

I contacted the guy who'd found Bambino, and he estimated the "considerable distance" to be about 35 feet. For a little 7-lb fawn that is not just considerable, it's humongous. When the Vet heard that, he said the jarring thud with which he landed, could well have splintered the bone, slightly torn muscles, tendons and ligaments connecting the bone to other parts of the leg, becoming a break just waiting to happen. One misstep or too much pressure on it, could cause it to easily break. The full implications of his statement didn't hit me then.

The Vet kindly sent one of his Techs to help me get Bambino to his office. He drove and I held Bambino on my lap wrapped in a blanket. The Tech had done the wrapping, to insure that the injured leg was held secure. During the whole ride, Bambino was quiet, calm, nuzzling with me on and off, the same sweet cuddly little guy he'd been from the beginning. He didn't struggle against me, but liked me holding him. The blanket and my holding him prevented the broken bone from moving around too much which might have caused him pain. I carried him inside where the Vet was waiting. It was 3 pm.

By 6 pm, Bambino had been delivered back to my barn by the Vet and his Tech. He was totally alert, with his leg cast and wrapped. They brought him into the stall, and the first thing he did was nuzzle with his stall-mate who had walked over to greet him. They were obviously glad to see one another. Then he nuzzled with me a little. The Vet and Tech left, after giving me my instructions.

I got their two bottles, warmed them, and at 6:30 they each had their 8 oz of milk side by side. He was able to maneuver around right well, and to even assume 'the stance' for taking his bottle. His appetite hadn't fallen off, fortunately, as it had taken us so long to get him up to 8 oz at a clip. There was little follow-up for me to do regarding his cast, but I did have to give him injections of 2 cc's of Penicillin twice a day. He didn't whimper about those, but as with everything else, he accepted it with no fuss and with a lot of courage for such a little guy.

This was Sunday August 2 of '98. With a cast, and needing extra room to maneuver around, he needed to have the stall to himself. So the other fawn, the little girl, had to be released suddenly upon Bambino's return from the Vet's that evening. Their 6:30 bottles side-by-side were the last they had together. I quickly debated the idea of moving her into the adjacent stall. This could present a whole new set of potential problems, not the least of which was that this meant my horses would have no place of refuge from storms. More than that, it couldn't be known how Bambino or she would react to being separated yet still being able to see, [through the small spaces between stall boards and the automatic waterer], hear and smell one another. If either tried to get to the other, it could have dire consequences. We'd already had one of those.

Releasing her was the only viable option, even though she wasn't ready to be released. This would definitely complicate things a whole lot more, because she still needed her 32 oz a day, and besides, they both needed to get started on solids. That meant keeping tabs on her, now free, and concurrently taking care of him, while he recovered. They'd been on the same feeding schedule, and that would have to be adjusted. Someone was going to get to eat earlier than the other. Separated, maybe they wouldn't be aware of that. I would find the way to make it work.

More than any of that, I felt badly for them both. They'd become such pals and now wouldn't be able to snuggle and do things together, wouldn't 'be there' for each other comfort-wise. That was sad because they each needed a friend, almost more than they ever had -- he because he was recovering, and she because she'd so suddenly and abruptly been shoved out of the nest. So they would both be dealing with another trauma in their young lives. They'd each had the loss of their mama, he'd had a significant fall, and she, well, you'll have to wait a bit to read about her initial trauma and her story, as she won't reappear until then.

Amazingly enough, the next morning his bowels were fine, and except for one other incident, they remained fine and normal. His appetite continued and he was getting his 32 oz daily. Now his leg just needed to heal.

Chapter 4

The next 2 ½ days went very smoothly -- his eating, going to the bathroom, getting up and down on his own and moving around the stall with unexpected ease and agility. His recovery seemed to be off to a good start. Giving him the Penicillin shots twice a day was no problem, whether he was lying down or standing. Either way he stayed still, didn't flinch or react in any way. Afterward I always patted and nuzzled him, and he'd return the nuzzlings.

I spent as much time in the stall with him as I could, and still took care of the other fawn now free, my dogs and horses, and other things in general. Often I spent the night in the stall with him, to monitor him, and help if needed. It also enabled me to see first-hand that he did sleep and sleep comfortably, which allowed me to do the same. In fact he slept through the night most of the time.

It took me back to nights with John Doe, and I'd forgotten just how cozy my barn and the stall are at night -- in Summer anyway. With the netting covering the stall openings, and all the other doors closed, one lamp lit outside the stall, the lights from the star coming through the cracks in the boards, the radio playing quietly, and country night sounds heard above it made for nice peaceful nights. Occasionally the horses' soft whinnies could be heard, adding to the overall peaceful atmosphere.

Something happened though, during the last half of that third day, August 5. I didn't know what, I only knew it was his leg, the one in the cast. He kept 'worrying' it is the best way I know to describe it, and couldn't stand or maneuver around at all. I called the Vet who told me to bring him right away, which I did, by myself. I pulled my car to right outside the barn doors, and opened up the passenger seat to its flat position, which made it perfect for him to lie comfortably. Then I loaded him and we were off.

I'd faced him toward me, and he rested with his head in my lap for the entire ride. The Vet had to do a second procedure as the first hadn't held. We were home by 10 pm. Once again, his spirits and mood were undaunted. He was hungry and at 11 pm had his bottle.

The Vet told me to continue the Penicillin shots, and then explained it was important to get and keep him moving little by little. In essence I was to be his Physical Therapist. He added to call him at any time. For any of you with pets, you know how reassuring that is, to know that help is only as far away as a phone call no matter the hour.

I've neglected to mention that I'd contacted my friend at the Deer Research Center when the first leg problem appeared, and had kept in touch with him. He concurred with everything the Vet had done, his procedures and protocols, and made a couple of suggestions as far as his rehabilitation.

One of these was to rig up a sling, to help him walk around without putting much weight on the healing leg, and to aid circulation in that leg. I still have the sling today. [I wasn't kidding when I said I keep everything.] The Vet-Tech came that night with a sling, installed the pulley and showed me how to use it. He also came over the next three days, often twice a day, to help me do the physical therapy. What a God-send he was.

Thursday August 6 Bambino was awake bright and early. I know because I'd spent the night in the barn, and he woke me up by nuzzling my neck. I lifted him up so he could go to the bathroom, helped him take a few steps, and then helped him lie down again. Although he really did this on his own, and somehow did it very gently, and cautiously, which was good to see, as I couldn't be with him constantly to supervise. There were times I just had to hope that he was managing ok if he got up and down on his own. I had put padding around the stall walls in case he lost his balance.

It was a gorgeous day, bright, sunny and warm, but not humid. After several excellent physical therapy sessions, in the sling and stall, I carried him outside and laid him on a blanket. This was his first time outside since he'd arrived eight weeks earlier. Fresh air in itself can give an additional boost to healing and recovery.

If things had gone well, he would have been being released at about this time. I couldn't dwell on that though, but stayed focused on his physical therapy which was his ticket to recovery, renewed health, and release. That was our goal, and when I say "our", I mean the Vet, me, and Bambino, because he seemed as determined as we were. He worked so hard and tried to do as I guided, whether in the sling or the short walks around the stall or outside, which increased little by little each session.

A friend had given me the little angel statue, which I'd put in his stall, and took with us whenever we went outside, just for fresh air, or for his physical therapy.

He had visits from his former stall-mate whenever he was outside. They were always glad to see one another, and would nuzzle and groom one another. This was harder for Bambino as he was lying down, but he hit whatever spots he could, and as she'd be leaning down grooming him, he could reach her face, ears and neck. It was nice to see them together again. Hopefully, he would heal and recover totally, and they could then be 'in the wild' together. That was a nice image to hold in my mind.

From Friday through Tuesday morning, the Vet Tech came practically every day, and as he'd done so often, sometimes twice a day. Each time he was more amazed at how well Bambino was doing, and how much progress he'd made and was making, in the sling, and in the walks around the stall and outside. He still needed assistance, but as with anyone in physical therapy, that assistance decreases as the patient's injury heals and their strength and stamina increases. That's just what was happening. The weather was still marvelous so the outside times were especially pleasant.

Chapter 5

All day Tuesday things had gone well. We spent a large part of the day outside, his P-T sessions had been productive, and I'd introduced him to a few bites of carrots and apples which he absolutely loved. About 7 pm I carried him into his stall.

I was giving him his dinner bottle at 7:30, when suddenly his good legs buckled and he collapsed onto the sawdust. I'd been supporting him, as he'd decided he wanted to stand up for his bottle, and somehow got my arms and legs under him as he fell so his fall was cushioned. He lay there quietly, and I bent down and nuzzled him to reassure him. As always, he nuzzled back.

Then he began craning his neck trying to get to his bottle, which I gave him right away and which he finished in no time. His front legs were folded underneath him, so they appeared to be ok. I didn't know if something in his cast leg was the problem again, as had happened before, or if God forbid, something else had happened. I only knew I had to call the Vet.

He met me at his office, and the Vet Tech he'd called in was the same who had spent all the time with Bambino and me. That was an extra comfort, for me, but also for Bambino as he knew him, was used to him, and felt comfortable with him. It was about 8 pm by then.

The first thing he did was take x-rays. I knew from the look on his face when he came to tell me what the x-rays showed, that things weren't good. It was a very bad break in the femur of his back right leg. He said that he would certainly do what he could, that he didn't want to give me false hope but had seen worse, and that this little guy was strong and a fighter. He added that he couldn't promise anything. I appreciated his candor, and he couldn't have been kinder. I could hope.

Then he said I should go home as it would probably at least several hours before he'd know what was what. He offered his office and comfy couch for me to spend some time with Bambino before I left, while he got everything ready. The unspoken words were understood by us both, but in his kindness and compassion, he knew he didn't need to say them. I put Bambino on my lap on the couch, and patted and nuzzled him. There he was again, nuzzling me. No matter what had come his way, and he'd had to go through a lot, he always had nuzzles to give.

Alongside feelings of hope, was knowing the potential reality of losing him. I didn't want to ignore that reality and not make this time with him extra special. I didn't want to look back and not have said the things I did, or not have said goodbye. So I prayed for him, and talked to him.

I told him what a trooper he was, how despite having more and more thrown at him, it never phased his spirit and determination, how much I loved him, and that he had a special place in my heart. I also told him that I would not stop praying for him, or hoping that we'd be back in my barn later, but that in case that didn't happen, his place in my heart was secure for all time even if this had to be goodbye for now. Believing as I do, that one day my pets and I will be reunited, helps. We had one last nuzzle, just as the Vet Tech knocked on the door to say the Vet was ready I gave his forehead a kiss just as I put him into the Tech's arms and then watched as he took him down the hall.

I'm sure the reader is far ahead of me. Bambino had to leave that night, August 11 into August 12, at about 1 am. The Vet called me while he was still under the anesthetic to tell me what he'd found, which was far worse than what he'd expected from the x-rays. We both decided that it was best to let him go.

A half hour later, the Vet arrived with my little friend in a nice box casket. I'd begun to dig a grave for him, in a spot near the barn. It helped me keep busy. He carried him to it and offered to help me bury him. I thanked him but declined. I've always preferred it to be just me and my pet, as hard as it always is. Twenty some years and many pet-burials later, it never gets any easier. But it's something I feel I owe them, for all they've given me. It's a last moment to share with just me and them.

Several days later the Vet called asking if I wanted to talk about what he'd found, and what his opinion was as far as Bambino's problems and the causes of them. I did, and it was very therapeutic and helpful.

In essence, based on the problems Bambino experienced, with bones inexplicably breaking, and his digestion, [and even though it had cleared up for the last couple weeks, the Vet felt it would have returned, and more severely than before], he felt it was all attributable to the fall he'd taken: that his overall bone structure had been badly compromised, and though impossible to determine which or to what extent until they actually broke, many bones had been significantly weakened, or slightly fragmented, making it only a matter of time before they broke; and that either through bruising or actual injury to his intestines and bowels, probably even his kidneys and/or liver, his digestion and elimination had also been compromised.

The procedures he'd used to try to mend his bones, ones that normally work, didn't hold, because as he proceeded, parts would fragment or disintegrate, leaving nothing to hold things together. So the 'fixes' didn't last -- they couldn't because of the fragility of his bones. The children's rhyme about Humpty Dumpty came to mind: "all the king's horses, and all the king's men, just couldn't put Humpty Dumpty together again." Sadly, so it was with Bambino. In his case, all the king's horses, and all the king's men, and one fine Vet, just couldn't put *him* together again. The fall had basically doomed him.

I think of him whenever I go to the barn. Once again a little fawn had shown me how to rise above circumstances, how to accept what comes and be of good courage even in the bad times, and how, despite them, to keep a gentle and humble spirit. Gentle, and humble, an undaunted fighter, my bravest -- Bambino.

Part V
Bambino's Stall-Mate

Chapter 1

This little girl, whom you met briefly and anonymously in Bambino's story, had been resting in a hay field not far from another fawn, likely her sibling, and her mama. A thresher began making its way through the field, jolting mama to high alert. She and her one fawn jumped up and bolted to safety. This little girl didn't have enough time to do the same, the thresher was too close. The farmer didn't see her until he was on top of her but miraculously the normally ruthless machine spared her, somehow sheering off only a small chunk of skin and fur from the top of her fanny, and slicing off the tip of her left ear. Now, for all you art buffs out there in reader land, what did I name her? Come on, think Impressionists. Yep, yep, you're a l ...m o s t... there. You've GOT it! Van Doe.

The above photo was taken before her rescuer contacted me. Pretty lush digs for a little fawn, eh? Good thing she didn't expect a cushy sofa when she got to my barn. She didn't seem to miss a sofa at all, and ensconced herself quite comfortably in the stall.

It was June 19, 1998 when she arrived, riding on the floor of the passenger side of the car of her rescuer. She was so little, and so quiet, just looking up at me as I peered in the window looking at her. Despite her obvious 'war wounds' from her battle with the thresher, on her back and ear tip, [which were healing nicely – in the photo, the small black area on top of her fanny is where she was gashed], she was absolutely darling, with those soft, kind eyes, the soon-to-be-grown-into ears, [even the one missing its tip], the dainty head, tiny but strong legs, and the tell-tale spotted fur. As with all the others, there was such a fragile look to her.

Experience had shown me though, that for the most part fragile doesn't mean weak. I'd learned the funny side of that from the battles of the bottle with Baby Buck, and the sad side of it from Bambino's compromised bones. From her size and weight of about 8 lbs, she would have been born around June 12 or so, making her about one week old -- just about the same age as her stall-mate Bambino, and they were just about the same size. As you know, they shared a stall until August 2. She was as friendly and outgoing as he.

And as you know, they became fast friends instantly, and did everything together until then.

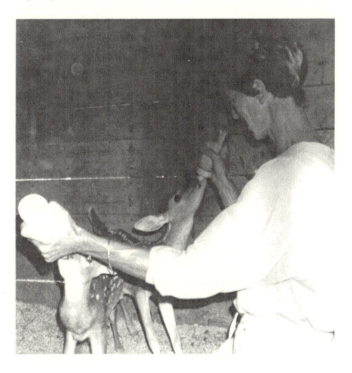

The veins visibly popping out on my left arm are further proof of just how firmly I had to grip the bottle against the strength of a guzzling fawn.

As I said in Bambino's story, when Van Doe arrived, I added her to the notebook, dividing each page into his and her records. That was easier than trying to keep records in two different notebooks. I included two pages from the notebook in Bambino's story. The following page is from July 30.

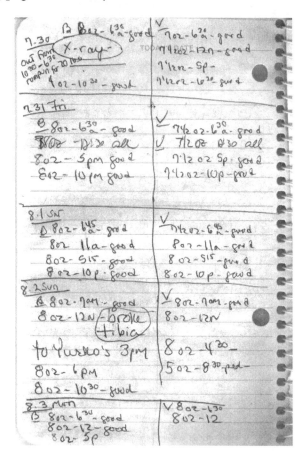

As you can see, Van Doe had just gotten up to 7 ½ oz per feeding at the end of July. The first two days of August she finally reached 8 oz per feeding.

Chapter 2

August 2 she had to be released because of what had happened to Bambino. The days immediately following her release, whenever I was outside, which was most of the time, with the dogs or horses, or on the way to or from the barn to take care of Bambino, she followed at my side wherever I went, except that I didn't let her come back into the barn as long as Bambino was there. That would present unknowns, and potential risks to each of them.

It was terribly hard to shut the barn doors in her face, that cute wistful face peering up at me, not understanding why she'd been pushed out in the first place, and why she couldn't come back in there now. She sometimes tried to push her way in with me. Unlike my bouts with Baby Buck over the bottle, I prevailed easily in this physically, but didn't fare so well heart-wise. I felt guilty and sorry for her, but knew it was the best thing to do. And she did adjust. She seemed to have decided, 'ok, I'll just glue myself to her side whenever I can', which she did - - and she became my little 'velcro-fawn' for many days.

Little by little though, she began venturing on her own around my property, getting to know the place, just as all the others had done. I'm amazed I didn't end up with more matching pictures of my fawns, like: John Doe in the front yard under the maple, Baby Buck in the front yard under the maple, Van Doe in the front yard under the maple... .

And since she'd decided to stick to me, keeping to her bottle schedule proved to be no problem. Actually, she was much like Baby Buck in how often she came in and how close she stayed. She would only become more-so as time went on.

Once I'd begun Bambino's physical therapy outside the barn, every time Van Doe came in when he was at the pine tree, she came to him there and greeted him. She'd lean down and nuzzle him, groom him, and just sort of be his companion again. If he was lying down, he would return the nuzzles as best he could, and make a stab at grooming her although he couldn't reach up very far. But they both seemed genuinely glad to see each other, and I always thought it gave especially him a lift. If he was standing and mid-therapy, she seemed to sense this and would go slower in her nuzzling and grooming. It was always a very touching scene.

There were a couple of times after Bambino was gone, that she'd go to the pine tree, and then look toward the barn, as if she was wondering where he was. Even though the main barn doors had been opened, and she'd always tried to push her way in with me when I'd be going to take care of him, she hadn't ventured into the barn on her own. Those first nights after he was gone, I'd left the outside barn lights and stall lights on, in case she wanted to go inside. I had told her he was gone, but two days afterward, August 14, I thought it might be a good idea for her to see that he was no longer there.

I used her bowl of grain and treats to lead her into the barn. She was tentative, but curious, and followed right along. After just a few bites, she went into the stall, and seemed to me to obviously be looking for him. She looked in every corner, walked the entire stall, sniffing all over it. As I watched her I talked to her the whole time and would have given anything to know what she was thinking.

When she came out of the stall, she passed by her bowl and came to where I was sitting on a bale of hay, nudging me, wanting to be patted and nuzzled. I didn't need to know what she was thinking, just that it had affected her to not see him there. She stood absolutely still while I nuzzled and patted her, maybe processing things, I don't know. After a couple of minutes she began to nuzzle me back, for another couple of minutes, then moved on, and walked to her bowl to finish eating.

A couple weeks after her release an old 'friend-of-fawns', Emily, came to call and brought her older sister. Emily showed Katie how it was done, and then let big sis have a go at it, but not without closely watching and supervising her. And you'll be reminded about the force with which a fawn drinks in seeing Emily having to double-fist the bottle and hold on tight.

And of course, there was still Baby Buck, in and out constantly, and here so much of the time. I'm not picking up his story here, not yet, though it is getting near the time when his and Van Doe's stories intertwine. When they do, I'll resume his story, and then return to Van Doe's.

Chapter 3

August 4 through August 14 were days of suspense, impatience, and near-agony for me. Baby Buck would come in, have his bowl at the bottom of the deck steps for instance, hang out for a bit, or not. He'd leave, maybe heading back down the driveway into the front field and across into the woods. Some seconds later, in would come Van Doe, from a totally different direction, have her bottle and food in the back yard, and head back in the direction from which she had come.

It was like those old Keystone Cop routines -- cops chasing crooks down hallways with more doors than you'd ever find in a real building, the crooks running in one door just as the cops were coming out of another one, and vice-versa and versa-vice and yada yada and on and on and on. I couldn't believe the near-misses these two were having. I think I even said so to them, along with things like, "you couldn't have gotten here like, fifteen seconds earlier? ten? do I hear five?" Hair-pulling time was just around the corner. Wasn't it Rudyard Kipling who said "east is east and west is west and never the twain shall meet."? Whoever said it, it came to mind. As did Robert Frost's "two roads diverged in a wood, and… I took the one less traveled…" These two kept taking the road the other *wasn't* traveling. If they'd *planned* it they couldn't have missed each other with as much precision.

But FINALLY! August15, 1998, they MET! Baby Buck had come in, eaten, and decided to stay. He and I were standing in the front yard, me patting him, when Van Doe came strolling around the corner of the screened porch. Ever waiting for THE Day, I always had her bottle with me when it was near feeding times. She paused only briefly, taking in the scene, decided things must be ok, and came straight to her bottle.

I kept patting him, and started feeding her, wondering how their up-close-and-personal, nose-to-nose meeting would go when I was finished doing both. He had his antlers of course, though in velvet as always, so I felt that even if they touched her, by accident or other, they wouldn't do her harm. I honestly felt that it would only be by accident that they'd come into contact with her, totally inadvertently on his part, and not by any design. Really, I didn't feel it was anything I need be concerned about for her sake. I knew my boy pretty well I thought. And I was right.

I also figured I knew my girl pretty well, and that even if her fawn exuberance took over and she 'jumped all over him', and I didn't seriously think there was a chance of that, she'd hardly make a big 'splash'.

As typically happens at those special moments, my camera was miles from where we were. There was no way to slip away and retrieve it. Besides, I wanted to just savor the moment. What a moment. A first. Two of my fawns meeting 'in the wild'. I can see it today, this very minute, clear as a bell. It's another of those images that gets indelibly etched in the brain and memory cells, never to leave or get lost.

The timing of their meeting couldn't have been better in my view, as it was just the day before that I'd shown her that Bambino was no longer in the stall. Once again, I had no doubt of God's hand in events. Not only did He know Van Doe needed something, He knew just what that something was, and was the only One able to send it to her. Of course that 'something' was my Baby Buck.

Picture two quiet, humble, friendly children, one about four years old, the other not yet one, meeting for the first time. The older will be especially doting, careful, and gentle; the younger eager to feel and touch, and investigate in response. The older might take hold of the tiny hand, initiate nose kisses and rubs, and the younger might grin with delight, and try to interact as far as their one-year-old skills allowed. Such was the meeting between Baby Buck and Van Doe. It was slow, sweet and soft. A photo couldn't have done it justice. They sniffed and nuzzled, and nuzzled and sniffed, for several minutes. They walked around each other, looking each other over, then started the process all over again.

I suddenly remembered how he did not like the velvet on his antlers touched. 'Hmm', I thought, 'do I intervene if she gets close to them?' I decided she'd have to learn that, as well as other things, on her own and from him, if they were to get along and become pals. And I knew I couldn't be there for all of that so I thought it best to remain just an observer. She did venture toward his ears, then his antlers, and *touched* one of them with her nose. I think I held my breath for just a second. He reacted as benignly as he had with me -- ducked his head out of the way and shook it a bit. She jumped back a little, clearly getting the message, then walked slowly toward him again, and steered clear of the top of his head altogether. My little girl was also a quick learner. This was a good sign, a show of respect, that she was alert to signals from him and would defer to him. I never again saw her get her nose even remotely close to his antlers.

I took a back seat, literally, on the deck step. They were on their own. I couldn't begin to know what was going through each of their minds, so I can only say that they seemed to take to one another from the start. Even though Baby Buck had a whole crew of friends 'out there', I thought that somehow this little one not only triggered some vestige of his Fatherly instincts, but also that in her he recognized a kindred spirit as he too had been an orphan. The latter may have been only from the fact that she began to follow him everywhere so it may have come through to him that she was alone. It's not important to know or guess why, or what the attraction was -- it only matters that from that afternoon on they were inseparable. What a pair they were, reminiscent of "Mutt and Jeff" for those of you old enough to remember them and their 'claim to fame'. For those of you not old enough, Mutt and Jeff were a funny sort of duo, with one of them huge and one of them small.

Chapter 4

As I was saying, Baby Buck and Van Doe became a team. It was hard to tell whether she was just persistent and insistent in following him, or whether he encouraged it and then she followed, but regardless, they each seemed to like the arrangement. As time went on, she was 'promoted' and they just traveled or browsed side by side. There were times when one would appear, seemingly alone for the time, but it wouldn't be more than half a minute before the other would appear, following the same path. Some times this happened at feeding times, but the one would be only seconds behind the other.

Most importantly, they genuinely liked each other, of that I'm certain. Many were the times I'd find them grooming one another, which isn't something just reserved for mamas and their fawns. It was so cute because obviously it was easy for him to lean down and reach her, but she had to do some stretching to return the grooming favor. And I never saw her get near his antlers again.

Not only did they end up eating beside one another, each out of their own bowl, but they even shared the same bowl many times.

The following photo shows just how well they got along, and that they made allowances for one another, the way friends do. In it, somehow Baby Buck had ended up eating out of the smaller bowl, Van Doe's bowl, and she from the big bowl, his. So it wasn't just that she being smaller, and out of respect for her elder, deferred to him. He obviously deferred to her at times as well, which was right in keeping with his nature. Not only had she finagled the big bowl, but then, the noive!, she began to poke her nose back into her own bowl, and his nose was already in it.

Baby Buck introduced her to his favorite resting spot in the front yard, the spot where the yard just begins its slight slope, where the maple tree affords some shade on hot afternoons, the one with the panoramic view, where he could look over his 'kingdom'.

It got to be routine, especially late afternoons, to find the two of them lying there together. I'd come up the driveway and see them there, or be home and see them out the window.

I imagine he introduced her to so many things, things I couldn't know about since I didn't travel with them. Thinking about that now, I'm not sure why I never did that. I could have walked right along with the two of them. Hmm, I don't know why I didn't. I guess I didn't think of it because they were here so much that I already got to spend such a great deal of time with them. Maybe that's it.

The feeding times were on a steady schedule. I'd hold Baby Buck's bowl as he ate, while giving Van Doe her bottle at the same time. When the bottle was empty, I'd get her bowl and then put both bowls down on the ground and they'd continue eating. They were just so cute together, I loved watching their interactions. I think he was equally glad for her companionship as she was for his. It's time now to resume Baby Buck's story.

Part VI
Baby Buck – Changing Seasons

Chapter 1

We're picking up Baby Buck's story where we left off in Van Doe's, September '98.

At first, Van Doe was merely Baby Buck's shadow, following behind like a little puppy dog. At some point, she got 'promoted', and their relationship evolved into a team who walked, ate, rested, and traveled side by side. They were good pals who obviously enjoyed being with one another. She looked up to him, not just literally, but figuratively. She took her cues from him, but she could also be independent and self-assured.

He became her friend, big brother, surrogate Father-figure, guide, teacher and guardian. If only animals could talk, I would love to hear all the things he had taught and was still teaching her about being a deer. In taking her under his wing, he may have begun his relationship with her as a big brother or surrogate Father-figure, but it seemed it grew into his enjoying her companionship for its own sake as much as she enjoyed his. Fast friends were they.

Soon it was September, and we had the bonus of a beautiful Indian Summer. Van Doe's spots were fading in mid-September and totally gone by October. Even though her coat was now like the adults, her size belied that she was a fawn, and not yet a yearling. That would protect her in the coming hunting season.

In thinking ahead about Baby Buck and the hunting season, I did all the preparations I'd done for the four previous seasons. Well, it was really only three since he was just a fawn himself for that first one in '94. I called my hunter friends, the ones who'd come to "Tea", contacted the adjacent neighborhoods, asking again that everyone keep a watch. Once again, everyone was so gracious and willing to help. They were all also glad to hear he was still with me.

Though I knew they didn't venture far, since he and Van Doe were traveling together, I needed to tell them all that he now had a little fawn who was with him practically all the time, so that they'd watch out for her too. I also had been checking the signs we'd posted, making sure that there were still plenty and that they were plenty visible. They were.

Sometime in September, between four trees just outside the fence of the pasture below the barn, I built a 'hut' for the two of them. I use the term 'built' rather freely. I wanted to provide a place that would protect them from the harsh winter weather, knowing that even if they felt comfortable going into the barn, the horses would likely be in their stalls-so no room in the Inn so to speak.

It wasn't so much that I really built anything. What I sort of threw together and affixed to the trees, was actually more of a triangular tented 'thing', using tarp for the 'roof' and half-walls on two sides. I made sure there was plenty of head room, considering Baby Buck's size and antlers. On the sides most exposed to bad weather and high winds, I extended the tarp to the ground. It was a fairly sturdy…lean-to, that's what it was.

I began using their bowls of grain and treats to coax them in while the weather was still nice. That way, by the time winter got here, they'd be used to it, and hopefully would seek shelter there. They both could fit, standing or lying down. I often chuckled to myself that I'd allowed plenty of head room for Baby Buck so he didn't have to 'check his rack at the door'. After I'd coaxed them in, they'd lie down for a rest and I'd sit down with them. One time I did end up in there with them when a sudden downpour came. Neither we nor the 'floor' got wet. Give my regards to the contractor.

And the luring worked! Several times throughout the rest of September, into October and November, when there were storms or heavy rains, and when the cold weather began, they were using it! It used to make me feel so good to see them going in, or to see them already in it when a storm hit. Short of bringing them in my house, it would have to do. And don't think there weren't times I didn't consider that, especially during hunting seasons. Count *those* double-or-triple negatives. Actually I think triple negatives are against the law. If not, they should be as they have me confused to the point that I'm wondering if it says what I mean, which is: I did consider bringing them inside - - at least into the basement, which *is* unfinished and I thought, what could it hurt?

The weather turned cold the beginning of November. Van Doe's coat had gotten good and thick, and she was 'fat and happy'. So was Baby Buck. With whatever forage they found in the woods, plus the food and treats they got from me, they were both in excellent shape to meet Winter. They kept up their same routines, their comings and goings, three to four times a day, and their 'stayings', though days with nicer weather were becoming less and less, so they didn't stay as long or in their usual favorite spot in the front yard. They'd hide out in some sheltered spot, like their lean-to , or I could see them hunkered down in the woods around my property. They were always together.

Beginning that day they first met, August 15, early mornings about 6, the twosome would arrive for breakfast. I tried to always be ready, but some mornings I was running late. I'd have just finished with the dogs or the horses, have put grain in their bowls on my way inside to get her bottle and their treats of carrots and apples, when I'd happen to glance out a door or window and there they'd be, looking in at me and waiting patiently side by side.

Interestingly, even though Baby Buck was very used to coming up on the deck to eat and did it often, he never did it at all once Van Doe and he were together. It seemed another example of his deferring to her in a way, in not leaving her alone in the yard.

Maybe he didn't think she could make the leap. Maybe he thought that since she didn't know where the can of grain was, why show her which might lead to her pre-empting him. He had gotten the lid off once and helped himself. I thought I'd fixed it so he couldn't do it again, but given enough determination he might have been able to. But maybe he'd not tried to open it since I'd secured it, and therefore thought Van Doe might be able to sneak up sometime when he was looking elsewhere and open it for a buffet of her own. Who knows. It just seemed an extra-gentlemanly, big-brotherly thing that he just remained in the yard with her. They often shared a bowl, which he never seemed to mind - - nor did she ever turn down the opportunity.

I'd go out to where they were, hold his bowl for him while I held her bottle for her. So often they stood not only side by side, but smack dab against one another. When she finished her bottle, I'd put both bowls on the ground and add the treats.

So from the day they met and became a twosome, this was how it went not only for breakfast, but meals at mid-day or late-day, and then evening at some point. The two were always in at least twice a day, more often three, and only sometimes four. The times varied, but it was usually 6 am, noon-ish, 5-ish, and around 11pm.

Of course once Fall arrived, it was dark by late afternoon, so sometimes they were harder to spot if they were just standing outside the door or window. I learned to put all the outside lights on, which I'm sure made the neighbors think I was always entertaining. In a sense, I was -- or more accurately, I was *being* entertained.

There were occasions too of course, that I just wasn't home, mostly the noon's or 5's. When I'd get home, if they weren't lying in the front yard or milling right around the house or barn, they'd be in within a couple minutes after I'd gotten here. I figured that when they had come in and I hadn't appeared with their food, if they didn't wait right here, they went somewhere close by to wait, where they could watch and see when I did get home. I tried but could never find that spot or see them coming from it. They would appear from a direction I wasn't looking, naturally. It must be one of the more obscure of Murphy's Laws: when you're looking for someone, they will always come from a direction other than the one you're looking.

Chapter 2

I should mention that Baby Buck's friend Lilly would often travel with the two of them. Obviously Lilly accepted Van Doe, and vice-versa, and the two had become good friends. They looked like a little melded family -- Big Daddy, Pretty Mama, and their Cute Fawn. It certainly did this 'mama's' heart good to see. It was nice, but meant I had to have three bowls on hand, or in hand. If Lilly were with them, I'd put a bowl down for her a little removed from where we were and she'd dine with them. It looked to me like a Disney movie waiting to happen. But then so much with my fawns looked like that to me.

November 3 through November 6 the weather warmed a bit, and each afternoon about 4:30 the three of them came and lay together in the front yard, Baby Buck and Van Doe in his-now-their special spot, and Lilly just a few feet away. They would chew their cuds, or just rest. Sometimes one of them would actually snooze a little. At least it looked like that as their head would be resting on their folded front foreleg and their eyes would be closed. Such a peaceful sight. Once they were up and stretching, which was usually around 5, I'd take out their bowls and the bottle. They had me trained well.

Late nights about 11 Baby Buck and Van Doe would often come, though I never saw Lilly with them. Perhaps in the darkness, she didn't feel as safe coming close, and just waited nearby for them. They never stayed long after they'd eaten at 11, just enough to get a few pats or trade some nuzzles.

One other revealing characteristic of deer, at least in my experience with them, true of Bambino and Van Doe when they shared a stall, true of Baby Buck and Van Doe, they never exhibited any signs of jealousy. One never tried to push the other out of the way for pats, nuzzles or food. Dogs certainly exhibit jealousy and will push other dogs and puppies out of the way for these or for attention in general. There may be other species who do this as well. And of course, we humans know jealousy. The lack of it in deer seems in keeping with their humble, patient, accepting natures.

November 7 it was back to chillier weather, and stayed that way through November 11. On those days the two were in four times a day, the colder weather making them hungrier. Lilly seemed to have taken at least a temporary sabbatical from traveling with them. Their 6 am, 5 and 11pm feedings were routine on these colder days, often skipping mid-days. For the 11 pm feedings, they'd come just inside the entryway of the barn to eat, and at this time of night when it was chillier, the horses were often in the stalls munching on hay. Everyone would eye everyone else, and go on eating, or in Van Doe's case, drinking then eating. Peace throughout 'the kingdom'.

And on it went, peace in 'the kingdom', idyllic and sweet. Until late afternoon November 12.

I've dreaded reaching this point, not knowing the best way to go about it. Easiest perhaps is to just put it up front. I lost Baby Buck that November day, the 12th, 1998. I was devastated. He'd survived four hunting seasons, but couldn't make his fifth.   In saying it, a flood of tears and heartache return as it all comes back, vividly. Now that the dread of putting it into words is past, I can go back and tell you about it.

Chapter 3

The morning of the 12th was the coldest one we'd had yet. Baby Buck and Van Doe were in as usual for their breakfast about 6 am. It was not yet light, so they dined by my outside lights. As always, I held his bowl while giving her her bottle. Then I put down both their bowls which they finished in about a half hour. With Winter coming, I'd upped their grain so it took them a little longer to eat. They stayed for another half hour or so, doing some 'pretend-browsing' in my yard. I was patting each in turn, and each began nuzzling with me. Then as always, they left together. It was just getting light.

To tell the truth, I don't remember how the remainder of the day went. I know they weren't in mid-day, which didn't cause great concern, as there'd been plenty of days when they hadn't come in at that time. At 5:15 pm, Van Doe came in alone. I've mentioned that there were times when one would come in ahead of the other, and the other would be only seconds behind. So for those first few seconds after she got here, I didn't think much about it. As seconds became minutes, and then many minutes, I could feel the fear in my heart grow.

I called him, which I've not referred to in awhile, but which I still did often just to bring them in, especially since it was hunting season. Once called, it never took them more than a few minutes at most to appear. I kept calling and calling him, and tried to stay optimistic, that he was just straggling longer, or ambling slower, or had gotten distracted. Deep down in those first minutes I think I knew, but tried to hold on to hope.

I tried to glean something from Van Doe's behavior, to see if she was showing any signs of stress or distress. She wasn't, and her coming at their usual late afternoon feeding time seemed at least some evidence of that. I think she drank her full bottle, and finished her grain and treats, but I wouldn't swear to it. I was becoming more distracted and worried, and didn't pay attention to whether she ate it all.

She stuck around for a long time, until well after dark. She lay down in the back yard next to her bowl, and his, which was still on the ground. That was the first inkling that was she was acting unusually. Normally they would leave soon after their late afternoon feeding. But perhaps it was explainable in that he wasn't with her so she stayed, waiting for him too. For a moment I thought, or hoped, that maybe she knew something I didn't, that maybe she'd gotten a whiff of his scent, and that he'd soon be in.

I grabbed a jacket from inside and sat with her. Every few minutes I'd begin calling him again. I kept patting her, and nuzzling her, and then about 8:30 she stood up and headed in the direction of the lean-to. She looked so tiny and lonely as she walked away in the dark. I tried to watch to see if she went into the lean-to, but the outside spotlights didn't reach quite that far. I hoped that was where she'd gone.

By this time I was frozen and shivering. I hayed the horses once more, and took my dogs for a quick play in the yard, trying to keep my mind occupied. It helped only momentarily but any distraction helped no matter how brief. I left all the outside lights on and went inside, to bed. I didn't sleep. It was a long terrible night. I felt so helpless. Every hour I was back outside, looking and calling. I thought of getting a flashlight and beginning a search, but didn't want not to be here when he finally arrived. I clung to 'when he finally arrived'. Finally daylight came.

Chapter 4

As dawn approached November 13, it was like the focus on a camera lens changing -- to see clearly I had to keep adjusting and squinting my eyes they were so tired from the night's vigil. I almost didn't even want to look in the yard, or scan the horizon or fields afraid of what I wouldn't see. I went about my usual morning routine with my dogs and then the horses. Then I fixed Baby Buck and Van Doe's breakfasts, got her bottle, went to the front yard and called them both.

Van Doe came around the corner of the screened porch and was at my side in five seconds. I had a feeling she had stayed the night either in the lean-to, or somewhere else right near the house or barn. She had her bottle, then her bowl, and ate every bite. The weather was beautiful, sunny and blue sky, and it was warmer. I kept calling Baby Buck, still hoping.

Other deer began appearing in the pastures and I'd strain to see if he was among them, but I knew he wasn't because he'd have come. Or I'd see a deer approaching from the distance, and my heart would soar, thinking 'finally, he's here!'. I had so many of those times throughout the day, it was torturous. I couldn't make myself stop being on the lookout for him. Van Doe stayed around most of the day. She was calm, and even lay down for a while in their favorite spot in the front yard. For some parts of the day, I sat out there with her, it was that warm.

About 10 am, I called a couple of the fellows, the ones who'd met Baby Buck at "Tea", to ask if they'd seen him yesterday, or if they'd been out in the woods that morning and seen anything. When I told them he'd not come in yesterday, their empathy was so genuine, they said "awww, no". They said they'd check with their buddies and if either of them had seen anything, they'd have them call. One of them did call, and said he had been over this far in the woods yesterday morning, to just the edge of where the Porters used to live, the property that abuts the huge expanse of woods, and seen a white truck just at dawn, that he'd never before seen up here.

I thought back to when Baby Buck and Van Doe had left yesterday morning, that it was just getting light. They hadn't headed exactly in that direction, rather around the end of the field, but I knew they often went that way and then toward those woods. I didn't know the folks well who'd moved into Porters', or their vehicles, and called them next. No, they didn't have a white truck; no, they hadn't seen one when they got up yesterday morning around 7:30; and no, they hadn't heard any gunshots.

I knew no one else up here had a white truck, but called each of them to ask if they'd seen one or heard anything. Same thing, they hadn't and all had been up by the same time that morning.

Now I tried to think back to whether I'd heard any shots yesterday morning. I didn't think I had, but I'd gone back inside after Baby Buck and Van Doe left, and with the cold the windows were all shut, the tv going.

The rest of the day I can only tell you that I played a game in my mind, trying to rationalize the white truck's being there, figuring that if it was gone by 7:30 that wasn't enough time to finish what they were doing and get their cargo loaded. I wouldn't even allow myself to call what they might have been doing by the right words. I also thought that if they'd been shooting, one of the neighbors would recall hearing that. I was desperately clinging to hope. I began to think something else may have happened to him, like one of those horrible accidents that I'd read about in the deer books. Then I blocked out those thoughts.

Chapter 5

As the day went on, Van Doe was sticking very close by, always within sight, if not right in the front yard. I raked some leaves for awhile, did some preparation for putting the flower beds to rest until Spring, and just putzed around, trying not to go crazy. At Noon, I got Van Doe's bottle, and the two bowls. Again I called him. I'd not stopped praying, and praying for a miracle. But he didn't come. Van Doe had her bottle, and grain, then lay down in their spot in the front yard. Having had no sleep, I didn't last long at raking, and grabbed a blanket for under me and went and sat beside her. We were there for the next 3 hours, though I'd get up and wander around calling and looking for Baby Buck. She stayed right where she was.

We were sitting there when I heard a car coming down our main road, from the direction of all the other houses up here, all of which are beyond mine. It was about 3 pm. I craned my neck to see which of my neighbors it was, and couldn't quite see. So I went up on my deck. By this time, whoever it was had passed well beyond my drive, [where there's a clear view of our main road], to a spot where I could just see the top half of the car which had now stopped. It was a white truck. I remember feeling frozen in place watching.

Someone was getting out, I could just see the top of a guy's head. He walked around to the back of the truck, opened and then a few seconds later reshut the top and lower half of the back hatch, slamming them shut hard. Jolted by the sound, I felt stunned as if someone had just punched me in the stomach and knocked the wind out of me.

I couldn't see what the guy was doing at the back of the truck. But in that instant, I knew. It was bad enough to know Baby Buck was truly gone. It was worse to see one of the creeps that had taken him. And worse yet to know he was in the back of that truck. Did I see him? No. I just knew he was in there. Without going into graphic detail, that you don't need or want to know, and I can't bear to explain, let's just leave it that they had to come back that day to get him to their truck, and had to stop on the road to adjust his position for whatever reason.

I raced to the phone to call my neighbors, hoping to find one of the men at home who would hurry and come with me to follow these guys and then what, I wasn't sure. They were poachers, of that I was sure. One of my hunter friends had seen the truck the day before, and certainly would testify to that. And I had photos to prove that the deer they had, was mine. Had been mine. Not one of the men was at home. In fact, no neighbor was home. I didn't think about following them alone, for a lot of reasons.

As an aside, for days afterward I tried, through a friend at the Sheriff's Department, to find who these creeps might be. I didn't know what I could or would do then - - it was so after the fact - - but I had to try something. He was never able to find the truck I described. My hunter friend hadn't gotten a license plate or make and model, and of course neither had I.

I'd thought that if I ever got the chance to tell these guys just what low-lifes they were, I would welcome it. I wanted to tell them I hoped they were horribly disappointed when they found his antlers were fakes of a sort, still in velvet, no trophy. I wanted to know if when they found he was neutered, did they feel the slightest twinge of sorrow or a hint of remorse, that they'd taken what was obviously a hand-raised deer, maybe even a pet. Logic told me that since poachers don't operate by the same rules or code of ethics you and I do, their hearts were probably just as cold as the metal of the guns they toted.

I would have wanted to tell them to stop kidding themselves saying they were sportsmen; that aside from the fact that deer, or any other hunted animals, have little chance with the high-powered weapons of today, guns or bows and arrows alike, this beautiful deer they took was so friendly he would have walked right up to them. Maybe he even did. [I'll speak about that a little later, because I had to take a large responsibility for it.] Yep, big "sportsmen". But my words would have been lost on them.

The afternoon of November 13, in that moment of knowing Baby Buck was gone, my heart stopped pounding and just broke. I finally had the emotional melt-down that I'd kept trying to stave off, but that had kept up its relentless pursuit. They say the world is filled with unlikely friendships, and ours was certainly that. But 'unlikely' doesn't begin to cover it.

For 4 ½ years, from May 21, 1994, through the morning of November 12, 1998, I hadn't known a day without him here. He'd become like one of the family, as my pets always are. I'd raised him from a tiny spotted fawn, and seen him through that, his release, his neutering, and four hunting seasons. And I'd come to realize he never stopped thinking of me as his 'mama', surrogate though I was. I think I felt much like a parent who has lost a child. That's not to say that losing a pet is equal to losing a child, but to me, it was akin to that.

I am figuring that anyone who picked up this book and started reading, and has hung in here still reading, is an animal-person, or perhaps a deer-person, at least a pet-person, in varying degrees, and has experienced the loss of a pet so understands how sad it is. That being said, I don't feel a need to explain or apologize for how I felt. I couldn't talk about him to anyone for days, and didn't want to. In fact it was weeks before I could, and when I did, I became devastated all over again. Such was the bond that had existed between Baby Buck and me.

Some time soon after he was gone, it hit me, and hard, why hadn't I tagged him? I could've so easily. I'd tagged John Doe; the procedure was simple and apparently painless to him, and I was fairly certain it had helped protect him. Sitting here today, I can't say why I didn't do the same with Baby Buck. I can't even say that I thought of it, because I just don't remember.

The other thought that followed this was, would it have mattered? I'm not sure, but I suspect not. Knowing it was poachers who took him, and knowing the inherent lack of ethics in poachers, I don't think it would have mattered to them had they seen a tag. I still wish I had done it though, because then I would know that I *had* done everything possible under the sun to protect him. It took me some time to get past my inexplicable omission. But at some point I had to let it go.

The other obvious question that arose was, did I let him get too used to people? I'm not sure that choice was mine alone, or that I chose it at all. I certainly didn't dissuade him from coming around, didn't discourage his hanging out here, but I'm not sure I'd have been able to had I tried. He may well have walked right up to the poachers, thinking they were safe. Circumstances led to his seeing me as his mama, since when he came to me he was at the vulnerable age when he was going to imprint and bond with someone or something in place of his real mama, and I happened to be the one.

Every human he came in contact with here was benign, so how could he possibly know about malignant ones? He couldn't, and for that I had to take responsibility, although I wouldn't have known how to present the other side to him even if I'd been able to foresee the future. The flip side of this was, that in his staying so close and being here so much of the time, it did serve to protect him for at least four hunting seasons. My place was a sanctuary for him, a respite from being hunted, and did keep him safe through those four hunting seasons. I had to hang onto those thoughts.

This same photo is in Van Doe's second section, and described there except for the date and circumstances. Though I didn't know it at the time, this was to be the last photo I would have of Baby Buck and Van Doe together. It was taken, serendipitily-enough, to coin a phrase, the night of November 11, 1998, the night before we lost him - - and for that reason alone I think it bears repeating.

In Bambino's story, I said that every time I go to the barn I think of him. When I pass the pine tree I used to carry him to for fresh air or physical therapy, or the spot by the barn where I buried him, he always comes to mind.

With Baby Buck, every time I go anywhere around my place I think of him, because he was everywhere, and all the time. But it's his spot in the front yard under the maple especially that evokes his memory the most. Right after he was gone I used to dream about him, and in the dreams he was lying there or under my bedroom window. Sometimes I can still see him in those places.

I hated that he was just gone so suddenly one day. Many times I asked God why I'd not been able to say goodbye to him. Some years later I would get an answer of sorts. For a long time after he was gone, his absence was profound. Gosh, I loved him so. As with any loss, my heart grew less sore as time passed. But to this day, I still miss him, his gentle presence and tender ways that always brought a smile to my heart.

We indeed had an unlikely friendship, but something beyond unlikely, beyond unique even. The joys of raising him from a tiny fawn, of being with him for the next 4 ½ years, the amazement that a one hundred-plus pound buck would invite me to play and share nuzzles with me through all those years, and the bond that became more cemented over those years, all this was a once-in-a-lifetime experience, a rare gift from God. I was so blessed, and privileged, to have shared 4 ½ years with so special and yes, enchanting a deer, my great friend, my fixture -- Baby Buck.

Part VII
Van Doe – My Noblest, Carries On

Chapter 1

Van Doe was always special, as were all my fawns, but with the loss of Baby Buck she became even more of a God-send. I felt even more grateful for her and her near-constant presence here which helped to fill the void I felt from his absence.

Then I realized three things: Van Doe and I had shared Baby Buck's last 3 ½ months of life; his being taken was sudden, stark, and blind-siding to each of us; and now we shared mourning him. What came to me next was that losing him had caused perhaps a bigger void for her, than the one I was experiencing. After all, I still had her. She didn't have him any longer. Realizing those things, I felt sadder for her than I did for me, which in its way helped my heart begin the healing process.

When Van Doe was just about one week old or so, she been run over and wounded by a big loud machine, and subsequently separated from her mama and sibling. Both of those would have been trauma enough. But then, when she was not quite eight weeks old, she'd been 'thrown out' of her cozy stall, and the barn, and that must have been exactly what it felt like to her - - thrown out. In there, she'd felt safe, she was cared for and fed, she had Bambino's companionship, [a replacement for her sibling], and mine, [a surrogate mama].

So she experienced another traumatic event in her young life. Suddenly pushed out into 'the world', she must have felt insecure, understandably so, and as evidenced by her following me everywhere, including trying to push her way back into the barn any time I went in to see to Bambino, and by sticking on my property or just barely off it. Although she did stay close by, and was in for her bottles right on schedule, for nearly two weeks she was on her own basically and did travel a little.

Of course so had John Doe and Baby Buck been, released and on their own, but the more I think about this, neither had had another fawn friend in the stall from whom they were suddenly separated. In John Doe's case, he'd come to me when he was considerably older than either Baby Buck or Van Doe, so perhaps he was less dependent. The bond he'd formed with me certainly hadn't been as strong as the one either of them formed with me, and that's why he was perhaps better able to become more independent and stay 'out there' once he was free.

Just now crossing my mind about John Doe is that with all he went through - -his broken leg and surgery, his digestion problems, and his neutering - - once freed he may have thought, 'Jeeeez, am I glad I'm outta there! What I went through! I'm steering clear of that place, and her [nice as she was]'. Surely he would have added that last.

Along came Baby Buck, or, along came Van Doe that afternoon when I was feeding Baby Buck, and finally after all those near-misses, the two had met. He pulled her under his wing that first meeting, and from then on they were the best of friends. In her eyes, Baby Buck came along and rescued her, and she and he became inseparable. Then, when just five months old, she'd had only three months with him, and now he was gone -- her best pal, her big friend who made her feel safe and taught her so much, her constant companion, had disappeared. Another major trauma in her young life.

Though I didn't see any outward signs of stress in her from her loss, either immediately after or in days or weeks to come, I knew that she must have been experiencing it, whether I saw it or not. Then something else struck me. Knowing how side-by-side they traveled, it was all too probable that she had been right there, either right next to him or very close to him, had seen her friend go down, and who knows what else. That had to have been hugely traumatic. It made me feel all the worse for her. And it made me doubly grateful to still have her, as I realized that she too could just as easily have been taken that same morning.

So all of that can certainly account for why and how our bond grew even more after we'd both lost Baby Buck. And grow it did. For a total of 5 ½ years she was with me, and especially after the loss of Baby Buck, she became as much as a fixture here and with me as he had been.

Now, lest the reader has already done the math, and is saying a little prayer, like: 'Oooh Lo- or-d, she was so good and didn't go day by day through the four years with Baby Buck, please, tell us she's going to do the same thing now with Van Doe and five and a half years…? We hope? Not that we wouldn't be fascinated, to be sure, but the paint's drying on the house and we so love to watch that.' Yes, yes, let me reassure you. We won't go through the days one by one with Van Doe. [I've already done some of them anyway, in her first section.] I held to that with Baby Buck didn't I? And since I see you're still here, I certainly don't want to mess with success and lose you now. I just did the math, and find it 'interesting' that I'm writing this in the year 2007, and Van Doe was with me 2007 days. Coincidence? I'm betting not.

Those first few days after we lost Baby Buck, Van Doe and I spent a great deal of time together, which undoubtedly helped forge the stronger bonding between us. Thankfully the weather stayed warm, since our time together was outside. I mean, it's not like she could come inside and sit with me in the basement or anything, right?

The photo below was taken November 15, 1998. She's in the front yard and to my way of thinking seems to be looking for Baby Buck. She's looking directly at 'their spot', where she and he used to lie. This may sound crazy, but I often wondered if she 'saw' him there as I had.

So much for waiting in the yard for her bowl. Maybe she just wanted to show me she could get onto the deck. Perhaps she had seen Baby Buck up there at some point and was imitating him, or she just did this on a whim. Either way, now she ate on the deck a lot, just as he had. If Baby Buck could see her now! As had been true with Baby Buck, there were times it seemed Van Doe was going to walk right up to the front door and knock. I can't honestly say it would have surprised me.

And then, Lilly reappeared, and she and Van Doe began to hang out together. I wondered if she somehow knew what had happened, or had even been near the two that morning and perhaps escaped a near-miss herself. Maybe she had come back to sort of step into Baby Buck's shoes in watching over Van Doe…? Or maybe she'd rejoined Van Doe because she too missed him and needed a companion. Whatever the reason, they became better friends, and began coming in together, and while Van Doe usually stayed, Lilly would head off soon after she'd eaten.

In another few days Van Doe took to lying in 'their spot' in the front yard. I wondered if lying there made her think of him more, or miss him more, if maybe his scent was still there, or if she thought that if she lay there, he might appear. I don't think it was coincidence that she returned to their spot. I think it meant something to her to lie and rest there as she and he had done so often, and I liked to think it comforted her in some way.

Chapter 2

I became more worried about Van Doe now, with poachers, and couldn't help but fear they might return. I determined to redouble my efforts to protect her. I called my neighbors and the ones on the neighboring hill, to describe her to them. Most said they'd seen her, and usually with 'the big buck'. They were so sorry when I told them what had happened to Baby Buck. I told them about the white truck, that they had to be poachers, as the only hunters allowed on any adjacent properties were ones I'd spoken with and they had no connection with the white truck. They promised to keep a close eye out for her, and for any vehicles or people that didn't belong.

One fellow said he would make a point of getting up earlier than usual for the remainder of the hunting season, to check their end of our hill. We formed a plan should a situation arise of finding odd vehicles or 'hunters'. Part of the plan was that if a vehicle was seen, he would alert me, and then he and another fellow would use one of their vehicles to block the main road, eliminating escape, except on foot. I would call the Sheriff and the Game Warden. They could trace them through the vehicle.

Then I called my hunter friends, my "Tea with Baby Buck" friends. I'd spoken with three of them, but hadn't had that final conversation with any of them. They were sick about what had happened. Not only had they 'met' him October '96, they'd seen and watched out for him through the next two hunting seasons. They told me they'd often seen the twosome, and said Van Doe was easily recognizable by her ear.

They also said they'd seen Baby Buck and Van Doe those first days of November, barely off Porters' old property and into the adjacent woods where they hunted, never far into those woods. They promised to keep an eye out, for her now, and for any odd vehicles they'd spot, as well as any poachers. They were very upset, not only for my loss, but about poachers gaining egress, and about giving decent hunters a bad name. Forget hunters, they give humanity a bad name.

I also called her in very often, and Lilly, several times a day, especially on those days when it was the kind of weather hunters like best. I kept this up until December 31, the last day of hunting season. On worst weather days of snow or winds, I led her into the lean-to with her bowl. Sometimes, though it took her a bit longer to come in, Lilly accompanied her and the two would stay in there for several hours at a clip.

Lilly wouldn't tolerate me in there with them, which I totally understood as she was wild, and had always been wild. She trusted and tolerated me for food, but that was the extent of it. She never let me pat her or get closer than about five feet before she'd back off or bolt. I learned that distance, and made sure to stop before I reached it. There were quite a few times when I looked out a window through the blowing snow to see the two of them in the lean-to. It was a sweet sight.

December 31, 1998, finally came and went, and Van Doe made it through, as did Lilly. As I mentioned, since my adventures with fawns began I always felt a huge relief when a hunting season came to a close. And I always said extra prayers of gratitude when my fawns survived.

The photo below is from early March '99, a very cold day. She's still in her winter coat which is doing its puff-up thing to keep out the cold. Perhaps you can see why the first time I saw this I thought she was having a major allergic reaction.

And when I didn't bring her bowl fast enough, well, like Baby Buck, she'd figured out how to open the can and just helped herself.

This is a favorite photo of mine. It's not as readily noticeable in a black and white photo as in the original color one, but that's a rainbow arching across Van Doe's neck.

There, see? True to my promise, we've just done 1 ½ years of Van Doe and me, in only a few pages!

Chapter 3

The summer of 2000, Sadie, my wonderful, wonderful Golden Retriever, developed cancer, inoperable and metastizing quickly. I first noticed it in her jaw, but when my Vet took x-rays, he found it was in her lungs. The prognosis was that her time was very short. I used some homeopathic remedies to try to ease any pain and her breathing. It helped for a few weeks, but all too soon we reached the point where it was time to end her suffering.

My God-Son Timothy, [whom you met in an earlier photograph feeding Baby Buck as a fawn], bless his heart, dug her grave for me. My Vet came July 12, and when Sadie was gone, he carried her down to her spot in the bottom of the front yard. I walked him to his car, thanked him, and when I returned to Sadie's grave to begin burying her, and saw what I saw, I had to first go get my camera. I couldn't quite believe what I was seeing.

I had never seen Van Doe lie in that front fenced field at all, let alone in the spot just below where Sadie's grave was. I was surprised yes, but more, awed. It took me back to the day I described earlier in the book, when the group of deer had arrived the day I had to have my first dog Mandy put to sleep.

Here many years later, a deer I'd raised from a fawn, came and 'sat vigil' while I buried my friend. I don't know what else to call it. I didn't speak to her when I first saw her lying behind Sadie's grave, but waited until after I'd taken the picture, afraid that she'd get up and come to me and there would have been no picture. It's nice to have it to share, although it's another of those images so etched in my memory that I don't need the photo to remember the moment.

She didn't get up at all when I quietly said hi to her, but stayed as she was. That too was unusual, on top of where she was lying. Her quiet presence was calming and comforting to me. I was sad and crying, but experienced a peace that I attributed to Van Doe's being with me and Sadie. It was an extraordinary moment.

It wasn't until I finished burying Sadie and started up toward the deck, that Van Doe left her spot and followed behind me. What she knew, how she knew it, and why she was there, who can say for sure? But I believe she was there for a reason, that she was guided there by God, and that she knew she was to stay there until I had finished.

It kindled warm feelings inside - - you know, the kind you experience when someone's done an unexpected kindness toward you. My heart was lightened even more when she walked beside me up the steps onto the deck. It was just like having a comforting friend nearby in a sad time. Granted, she was interested in some food from her can. But that's what friends do too, right? Come to call and happily partake of 'vittles' or 'potables'.

There are plenty of documented and everyday examples of animals who sense things far beyond what we humans have the capability or capacity to sense. Witness bomb-sniffing dogs, assistance dogs who guard and guide those who can't see or walk, dogs who are able to alert their owners to impending seizures or heart problems. Consider dolphins who inexplicably single out people with cancer or other serious illnesses to interact with them, to the exclusion of other people near, which gives these people such an exhilarating feeling and experience; or horses used in programs like "Ride with Pride" who instinctively know they must be extra gentle as their 'cargo' is precious -- children who are blind, severely handicapped or even amputees.

These animals come to our aid, and *are* our aid, time and time again. Who's to say that deer too don't have these same innate qualities and senses? After what I witnessed, back in '88, and again in 2000, I have no doubt that they do possess them. The group of deer that snowy day in February '88 who sat on the hillside looking toward my house when I had to lose Mandy, and Van Doe who took up a spot just below where I buried Sadie, I believe, were sent or guided to those spots, for a mission. They were as much of an aid and comfort to me those two days, as are any of the animals whose gallant feats and everyday kindnesses touch the lives of those in need of help, a special touch, or an unforgettable experience.

As I think back to all the different children that came over the years, who met John Doe, Baby Buck, and Van Doe, I see these fawns have already made a case for the therapeutic effect deer can have. To wit: the one little boy who was so stern at first but whose glower turned to smiles with just a few sniffs and licks; my nephews who didn't stop grinning the entire time they got to interact with any of my fawns; the Day Care kids who even at their young age were thrilled to have such close contact with another 'young kid'.

I shouldn't limit this to children, as over the years there were plenty of adults who loved coming to my barn to meet the newest arrival. One summer afternoon in '98 I had about eight friends for lunch to celebrate one friend's birthday. Most of the group that came got together on a regular basis to do this, but one of the gals wasn't a big fan of 'lunch with the girls' and came rarely to these gatherings. She came out to the kitchen at one point, so I asked her if she wanted to see something special and took her to the barn to meet Baby Buck. She was so taken with him, and said afterward that it was the best part of the luncheon and afternoon.

Chapter 4

Back to Van Doe, summer of 2000 and some extra-fun days. I'd suspected it for some time, and then June 16, I got my first viewing and visit!

Van Doe had a little one of her own! Her tummy had begun to look rather large in May and more-so in June. I kept hoping she was pregnant, but by about June 12, when other does had been coming to the back field with their fawns, and she hadn't appeared with hers, I thought either she hadn't been pregnant or her fawn hadn't lived. So it was such a celebration that day she brought in her fawn! The next generation of Van Doe's! I felt like a first-time Grand-Mother!

From its size and abilities walking and following her around, she was about two weeks old -- just the time when the fawn is supposed to start traveling with mama and learning all sorts of deer things. So the little one seemed to be right on schedule.

Then I began to get a little confused, as the fawn's 'eyebrows' seemed to change shape now and then, or from day to day. The confusion was cleared up one afternoon when I saw two fawns with Van Doe!

Their different-shaped eyebrows helped me distinguish between the two. I named them Annabelle [on the left] and Doesidoe [on the right], and talked to them hoping they would get used to me and venture closer to me. They never really did get very close, except with mama as a buffer between them and me.

But they did get more used to me, and wouldn't bolt when I'd come to bring Van Doe her bowl, or just visit with her. They did always keep one eye on me though, while they browsed. I think I've neglected to mention that it's very common for a doe to have twins, almost as common to have triplets, and fairly unusual to have just one.

They were both little girls and Van Doe knew it was safe to bring them in to meet me. I felt honored. They followed her into the front yard but often hid behind her, steering clear of me. They reminded me of Lilly who had hidden behind Baby Buck those first days, and then finally ventured out from behind his fanny. They too eventually realized I was no danger to them, but those first days I saw only parts of them - - an eye, or an ear or a couple of legs.

In fact Van Doe really never missed any feedings, usually coming in early morning, then mid-day, late afternoon, and late night around 11 pm. Her fawns were sometimes with her, but not at the late night times. She still enjoyed getting patted, and nuzzled by me, and as always, would return the nuzzles. During the days, her fawns would stick around a bit, then when she lay down in the front yard, or wherever, and I'd sit with her, [which I did no matter how cold], they'd go down into the front field and rest themselves.

The spot she picked in the front yard was always the same one she and Baby Buck favored. I loved sitting with her, and sitting in 'their spot' with her. Sometimes I'd find her there at feeding time, just sitting and resting, even on days when the weather was cold. I'd look down in the field and just be able to spot a few ears -- her fawns. I'd give her bowl to her, and sit with her while she ate. They were such peaceful special times. Annabelle was fairly brave when on the deck with mama, but watched me closely.

Van Doe was a good mother, very doting with her little girls, who were now becoming bigger and losing their spots. She was always grooming them and being affectionate with them.

Finally I caught it on film - - Van Doe leaping onto the deck! December '00.

Winter had come. Snow was falling and flying, and the temperatures were chilling. By this time the fawns coats had become the grey-brown adult fur, and I had a hard time telling the two apart. They had also developed the thick dense coat, as had their mama. To all appearances, the two seemed to be thriving extremely well, despite the harsh weather.

They had gotten totally used to coming on deck to eat. I never saw both come onto the deck at the same time to share Van Doe's bowl -- they seemed to take turns. She never seemed to mind when they poked their heads in her bowl to partake of the goodies. At least I never saw her push either of them away from the bowl. I wondered if it reminded her of the many times when she pushed her way into Baby Buck's bowl and how accommodating he had been to her. Perhaps this was another lesson she had learned from him.

I don't know what became of Van Doe's fawns. One day starting sometime in February 2001, they simply were not with her. Whether some horrendous accident befell them, or she drove them off early in preparation for the next fawning season, I never knew. But I always wondered. I wondered too if Van Doe had been with them, had witnessed yet another tragedy, or sad event that she didn't understand, and therefore experienced yet another trauma in her life.

This is the last time I saw Annabelle.

Chapter 5

At the beginning of each hunting season, '99 and 2000, I contacted all the same folks to ask for their continued help and look-out for Van Doe, and her fawns. I did all the same checks of the posted signs, and kept calling her in. The end of hunting season was always a joyful time for me. Once again, they made it through safely.

2001 arrived. In May the 'Maternity Ward' in my back field was *filled* with soon-to-be-mamas. I felt like I was running a birthing clinic. At any given time of day there would be from two to ten pregnant does milling around in the back field. It was quite a sight. Often several would lie down and rest, and the others would continue to browse. And sometimes the entire group would lie down to rest.

Among them was Van Doe. This time there was no mistaking that she was pregnant. It was exciting, and I was so happy for her after the loss of her first-borns. She was fit, and healthy, and eating like - - well, a horse. Van Doe would browse with the other pregnant does, but eagerly gobbled up her bowl of goodies, which I increased to accommodate her larger appetite.

Van Doe had just one fawn, which I first saw 6 am, June 26, '01. Again I felt like an honorary grand-mother when she brought her little one in to meet me.

She was darling, and tiny, just like her mama had been. I named her Doedie. She wasn't the least bit hesitant to follow mama onto the deck, but was leery of me. Look closely at the photo below - - you can just make out her head peeking under Van Doe's neck. She did get more used to me as time passed, and even got to the point where she'd let me pat her. That was going to be very useful later.

Once again, Van Doe was a wonderful mama. She spent a lot of time grooming and licking her, nuzzling with her. Such scenes were always mesmerizing for me to watch.

But she and I still had our special together-times.

I'm not going into detail about it, but Doedie developed or caught some virus or intestinal bug. I tried getting medicine into her via her food, as she'd gotten used to having a bowl on the deck. It was somewhat successful, partly because she'd grown less leery of me. I also was able to get a few injections of Penicillin into her. I had to be super-quick, with barely time to aspirate, but I managed somehow. She had just become used to me, and I hated pricking and scaring her. She kept coming back on the deck with mama though, so at least she got over her fear of me.

And I kept trying, with the meds and shots, but she was not getting any better, or thriving. I'd spoken several times with the local deer expert, and my friend who ran the Deer Research Center at Penn State, and was doing all that they suggested. Since she was wild, I was limited in what I could do. It just broke my heart to see her and know that short of a miracle, she wasn't going to make it.

November 6 she did not come in with Van Doe. It was so sad because it meant she was gone. Another trauma in Van Doe's life. In retrospect, because of her start in life without her real mama for the full time a fawn is normally with and nursing from mama, perhaps Van Doe missed out on some vital nutrients, such as colostrum, so vital to fawns and their immune systems, [and puppies, and maybe other species]. Maybe Van Doe never got it and other nutrients that get passed on from mama to fawn, that were important not only for her as a fawn, but for her when she had a fawn of her own, to be able to pass them along. I don't know and never could find an answer for sure. Considering that her first two fawns just suddenly weren't with her any longer, it seems plausible that they too had succumbed to the same immune system compromise. Doedie was the last fawn Van Doe had.

Chapter 6

Hunting season '01 brought the same concerns of the previous ones. I went through all the same precautions, checking signs and contacting everyone. And as always, prayed throughout it for Van Doe and Lilly. As had become routine, I called them in lots, in an effort to keep them close. And it worked well as they were here most of the time, often taking refuge in the lean-to. I kept being amazed at how sturdy that little thing was, defying the ridiculously strong winds that come up our hill. I also prayed for the 'regulars' who spent so much time here.

Van Doe and Lilly made it through another season. January 1, 2002, I called my hunter friends and neighbors on my hill and the adjacent one to tell them the good news, and thank them for all their help and watchfulness. Everyone was always glad to hear that they'd been unharmed.

We were into another hunting season. Once again, I made all the calls and contacts, checked all the posted signs, and called her and Lilly in several times a day. And once again, it was a nerve-wracking time for me as they'd all been. December was horrifically cold with a lot of snow, just the sort of weather hunters like. That added to the worries. And those poachers were always in the back of my mind. The lean-to was still up and I spent several freezing afternoons in there with Van Doe. When Lilly came, I'd scoot out as unobtrusively as possible. She'd take my place.

December seemed to drag, maybe because there were so many grey snowy days. But finally, December 31 arrived. Van Doe was in early in the morning, with Lilly. Around noon, they were in the lean-to and I took their bowls there. They stayed there for a few hours and then the next time I looked, they had left. I began calling them about 4:30 that afternoon, and it didn't take long for both of them to appear -- maybe two minutes, so they must have been close.

I think they were extra hungry because the day was so cold. Lilly left before Van Doe, and walked in the direction of the lean-to, though I couldn't see if she went inside it. Van Doe hung around until it was just turning dark, then she headed to the lean-to. I hoped she'd gone in, and that she'd found Lilly there.

Another hunting season had ended and my 'little girl' Van Doe and her friend Lilly had survived! It was Van Doe's fifth. At 8 pm, I bundled up again, filled their two bowls and headed toward the lean-to, calling them. And there they were all toasty warm and safe!

About 11 pm I put on all the outside lights, and they were waiting in the front yard. I bundled up once more and headed outside to give them their bowls. The wind had died down which made it more bearable for all of us to be out in the weather while they ate.

They headed back toward the lean-to in the woods. I headed inside, heaving another sigh of relief and sending another prayer of thanks heavenward.

The next morning January 1, 2003, 6 am, Van Doe was waiting on the deck. I didn't see Lilly that morning but that wasn't all that unusual. She came sporadically and often would not be around for several days at a time. I didn't see her for the rest of the month.

But Van Doe's routine didn't change. From that morning through January 4, she was in, mostly on the deck, or in the front yard, three or four times a day. The weather was warmer, at least it was above freezing, and the days would soon begin to lengthen, encouraging signs that Spring was getting closer and closer. We still had some Winter to get through, but that first day when it's no longer dark at 5 pm is so welcome.

Her appetite was good, and she'd stay around, sometimes lying in her spot in the front yard. I sat beside her as I often did, and talked with her as I always did. I'd pat her, and stroke her fur and ears. She always had loved her ears being stroked especially. And I always loved putting my hand down through her puffed-up coat to feel how warm she was underneath. If my hands were at all cold, a couple of minutes 'in' her coat and against her body and they were back to warm.

January 5, Van Doe didn't come in at all in the morning. She didn't come in all day, though I spent a lot of time calling her. And I walked all around my place, over toward the neighbors and the woods, calling her. I was worried, but optimistic. After all, she'd made it through hunting season, her sixth, so she was safe. The next day was a repeat of the one before, and I couldn't imagine where she was. I thought maybe she'd met up with Lilly and followed her wherever it was that she went when she'd not be here for several days.

Then I thought maybe she'd gone off with some handsome buck, though that didn't seem too probable -- not unheard of, just not probable. Rutting or breeding season had come and gone. Though I have seen what the books say proved wrong, at least up here on our hill and in my fields, that does and bucks do not congregate together or socialize except during breeding time, I hadn't seen just a single doe and buck traveling together after breeding time. I was running out of possible realistic scenarios, and with each passing day, it was harder and harder to stay optimistic. I could feel my heart sinking lower each day.

Chapter 7

Finally, about 8 am January 10, in the middle of the worst snow storm we'd had in a few years, I was at the kitchen sink and saw a deer come and lie down next to the dog pen. It was such a driving snow I couldn't make out if it was Van Doe, but I threw on winter gear and got out there as fast as I could.

It was Van Doe and I was elated! I threw my arms around her neck and hugged her, asking her where in the world she'd been, telling her how worried I'd been. About 6:30 that morning I had been outside calling and calling her for a long time. I'd walked to the edges of my property in every direction, looking and calling. With no signs of her, I had come back inside frozen, wet, and disheartened. To have her back at last was an answer to prayer.

When I moved back from her a little to have a good look at her, I instantly knew she didn't feel well. Her eyes said it all. She looked like she'd dropped quite a few pounds, and her coat was matted down in a couple places, not puffed up as it should have been for the day's weather of blowing snow and cold temperature.

I had prayed that she be brought back to me, but this was certainly not the answer I'd sought. I can remember thinking 'Lord, not like *this*.' I can't describe all the feelings that began clamoring inside me. I can barely put the words down as the feelings grab at my throat and the scene comes alive for me.

I ran back in the house, panicked and afraid, grabbed blankets, several heavy winter parkas and a couple of scarves. I covered her up as best

I could to hopefully warm her. I had put my hand down through her coat and her body was not warm as it should have been.

Then I began a methodical search for any pain or injury, or for the cause of her obvious physical distress. I found it. She was bleeding, profusely, from her hind end. I won't go into detail as it would serve no purpose. If I'd only seen her coming sooner, maybe I could have intercepted her near the barn and guided her in there and out of the horrible weather. If, if, if. All those sorts of thoughts began racing through my mind.

I called our local Zoo, so grateful a couple of the deer folks were in at this early hour, and told them what had happened. I described every detail about her injury that I could, but said that I couldn't exactly determine what was what as I was afraid to cause her further pain by any probing examination. I described how she seemed and looked, the state of her coat, and that her body temperature must be fairly low.

Their words devastated me. There was a virus, highly contagious and rampant among the local deer that Winter, severely debilitating, painful intestinally, and fatal. I almost couldn't believe what I was hearing.

It took a few seconds to take it in and realize what had to happen. They said how sorry they were, and I called my Vet. Thankfully, I caught him before he'd gone to his Clinic, and as always in any of my emergencies, he said he'd come as soon as he could. I prayed he would be able to get up our hill, which can be notoriously difficult in Winter. He said he would get to us if he had to walk. That's the kind of fellow and Vet he is.

My goal became to keep her as quiet, warm and comfortable as possible. A million thoughts and ifs were screaming in my head. Foremost was, why in the world, after surviving six hunting seasons, and so many traumas before that, did she have to be stricken with this? How, when she was here so much of the time, did she catch this deadly virus? [the answer to this was obvious from all the deer that travel through here] And how, in her obviously weakened and sick state, had she managed to come in?

Worst of all was, had I missed her, missed seeing her, that morning or the days before, as I walked around, looking for her? For days afterward, I would mentally replay every path I took in those searches, and interrogate myself over and over as to whether I'd looked carefully enough, there, or there, or *there*.

Chapter 8

I sat beside her for what seemed like eternity, patting and stroking her, especially her ears as she always loved that so much, and talking to her, trying to impart a sense of calm to her, despite what I was feeling. I know animals can sense fear and upset in humans. I prayed for her, with her. After about ten minutes, she struggled to stand up, and I tried to help steady her, though I wished she had just stayed where she was.

She headed over toward the woods just beyond my driveway. There was nothing I could do but go with her, and hope she would not go far. I grabbed the blankets and coats, and she lay down about fifty feet into the woods. I honestly don't know how she made it that far, though I tried to help her. Thankfully, I got a couple of the down parkas under her, and a few of the blankets were still dry so I covered her up again. The wait continued.

Somehow the Vet got his truck up our hill, though he had no snow tires. When I heard him coming, I had such mixed feelings, gratitude and dread at the same time. I called softly to my Vet so he could follow my voice and find us. Van Doe was lying peacefully, against me and a fallen tree, with her head in my lap. He stopped some 15 feet from us, and whispered that he'd brought a sedative to use first, and that it would put her into a semi-conscious state. We decided it might be best that I give it to her, so his coming next to us wouldn't startle her. That way, with just me next to her, she would feel calm and totally safe, and as it took effect, I could talk to her and say my goodbye with just her and me.

I don't know that I have ever done anything as emotionally difficult. But I did it, for her, to stop her suffering and let her drift away peacefully. Thankfully, the needle going in didn't make her flinch at all. I told her she'd soon be with Baby Buck again, and her fawns, that I loved her so and would miss her terribly. I leaned down to nuzzle her, and as weak as she was, as lousy as she felt, and with the shot beginning to work, she nuzzled me back. I'll never forget that moment.

The sedative took full effect very quickly, and I nodded to my Vet. He came to us, knelt down, put one arm around me and his other hand on her head, and prayed for her, and me. Then he gave her the final injection. Van Doe was gone.

I covered her head, and made sure the rest of her was covered. We walked back to his truck, I thanked him, and after a few minutes, he made his way back down our slippery hill. After he left I really broke down, and allowed myself that catharsis. Actually, I doubt I could have stopped it.

I couldn't bear the thought that she'd lie out there unburied but knew I couldn't dig in this weather or through frozen ground. A friend called a fellow who did miscellaneous work for her, and he offered to come, despite the weather and out of the goodness of his heart. I'd met him once, and he was one of the gentlest souls I've known. He came, and I walked him over to where she lay. I lifted the blanket covering her face to see her once more, then patted her and said a silent second goodbye. He said he would have no trouble, and would just leave when he was finished. I thanked him profusely, and he gave me a hug. I headed to the house, drained.

In the days afterward, time and distance from the loss of Van Doe, began easing my sadness, and helped me reflect on some things. As I intimated somewhere in the beginning, getting to say goodbye can be a mixed blessing, a double-edged sword. Saying goodbye to Van Doe was certainly that. But after Baby Buck, I remember asking God time and again why I hadn't gotten to say goodbye to him. So I got my goodbye with her.

In essence I'd asked for it, and had to be thankful it was granted. It would have been horrible not to know what had happened to her, yet it was horrible to see her in that condition. And at the same time, I had to feel grateful that I, or, the Vet, could stop her suffering. It was so tragically ironic that she survived six hunting seasons, only to then get this fatal virus. A few days later I made a plaque for her, with her name and dates on it, and nailed it to the fallen tree next to which she's buried.

I ran across this in Van Doe's album, apparently written the day I lost her, although I had forgotten about it: "Every 'animal' it has been my good blessing to know, and sad task to sit beside when their time to leave this world has come, has done so with a quiet nobleness and humble serenity, that I would aspire to emulate when my time comes. January 10-'03-the day I lost Van Doe."

I believe Van Doe came to say goodbye, that she was led or brought back for that, and that it was as much for her sake as mine -- hers, that she would be freed from her suffering, and have the comfort of being with me; and mine, that I would get to comfort her and say goodbye. Our answers to prayer may not always be what we plan or hope for, but there are blessings in the midst of ones we don't fully comprehend or appreciate at the time.

She was such a gentle friend, with me from June 19, 1998 through January 10, 2003. They were an extraordinary two thousand and seven days. Despite all her losses, that were many and significant, remarkable in her resilience she forged onward, with grace and acceptance, and in her final moment had nuzzled me back in friendship and strength -- such was the nature of my noblest -- Van Doe.

EPILOGUE

This remains a wonderfully peaceful spot up here on my little hilltop. The deer still come regularly. They meander through, stopping to browse or rest in my fields, yards, or barn. I still greet them all, and talk to the ones who will tolerate it without bolting. The 'Big Boys' still congregate in the fields, and especially around mating time they're 'struttin' their stuff' and 'checkin' out the chicks'. Come early Spring, the mamas still bring their newborns and secrete them nearby, often in the front field 'Day Care'. Sometimes they deposit them even closer, just on the edge of my front yard or next to the barn. The mamas are used to me and realize that I'm 'safe', so they're often found lounging in my yard. It's nice receiving their seal of approval.

On its first trip with mama into close proximity with me, a fawn is such a source of amusement and entertainment, doing a great imitation of Chicken Little. It bolts and darts, starts and stops, leaps and races around in circles, all the while trying to get mama's attention: 'HEY! Don't you SEE? We got Trouble-with a capital T! Who's THAT? What're you doing so clo-o-o-ose to her? Are you just going to STAND there!? She's right THERE! Aren't you going to RUN?! C'mon, let's go! What are you do-ing? Mom! YO, MOM! Ma-awm…?' Out of exasperation at getting nowhere with mama, or out of exhaustion from all its exercise, and most likely both, the fawn ceases its frantic activity and skids to a stop.

It stares at mama, then at me, back at mama, walks over to her and glues itself to her side. You can practically see it trying to figure out how to cover its tracks and now be the epitome of calm: ' yeh, well, um-uh, only kiddin' ma… I was just practicing my dodges and leaps…staying on my toes, er, hooves…you always say it pays to keep in shape…I know, everything's ok….ev-ery-thing…is…O-K. okey-dokey. yep. yeppers. I'm ok…you're ok…s h e' s o k. I knew that. Sooo, where're we goin now? ahh, we're stayin here a bit hunh? Wellll, okey doke, this is good… staying a bit is good…yep, it's O-k…we'll just hang here some more and be just fine… yep, we'll be okey dokey.'

Eventually the fawns learn that I really am ok, and soon they're meandering through with mama just as calmly as she. Sometimes they even lie down with mama in my yard. As they become more and more used to me, I talk to them, sharing things like: "I've had a little one like you -- actually five little ones, just as cute and pretty [or handsome] as you, but my goodness, they never carried on so. You're wild though, so I understand. But listen, you never have to worry about me, 'cause I just *love* little ones like you." Shades of all my fawns echo, as this or that wild one watches me intently while I talk, and seems to be listening, as if it's catching on to what I'm saying. Shades and echoes, reminders and memories of my old friends tug at my heart. I suspect they always will.

The endings of Bambino's, Baby Buck's, and Van Doe's stories were sad, and still put a lump in my throat. Not to sound cavalier, because the loss of each was devastating at the times, but as with people so with my fawns -- it's not their dying and loss that matters most or that's to be most remembered or dwelt on, because that's not their essence. It's their living, their being, and what it brought to my life that most counts, that's most remembered - - that's their legacy. I think of all my fawns, a lot. It would be next to impossible not to and still live here, still enjoy the outdoors as I do, and still love the deer who come. But it's with the happy memories of the good times that I think of them.

Inevitably, the same thought returns every Spring -- what if the call comes today asking could I take in a fawn? 'Could I?', I think to myself. Certainly, I could -- the barn's still standing, the netting and wire fence are still intact, the kit with the supplies is in the hall closet, and now that I've found and pulled together all my old notes and information, they're all readily available. So, while I know I could, would I?

I suppose it would depend in part upon the circumstances, how dire the situation, if the fawn is injured or ill and how seriously, whether it's fixable or curable, and what the prognosis might be. Of course the catch is, the answers to some of these are only revealed once the raising has begun. I know that it would present a real dilemma - - the old 'heart-vs-head' struggle. In all honesty, without very clear direction from God that I'm meant to take in another fawn, I think my response to such a call would be to offer to help walk them through raising it, to even be 'on call', and to loan them whatever supplies I could.

A side issue is that apparently our state no longer certifies lay-folk to rehab wild life, deer in particular. [not that there was ever any formality to the certification.]. While that wouldn't prevent me from doing so if I felt it were something I was truly meant to do, it might intimidate someone else. In that case, I have a friend in a hilltop neighborhood nearby who has taken in a few fawns over the last couple of years, that I could refer them to if, for whatever reason, they didn't accept my 'walkthrough' offer.

So while I know I *could* raise another one, my overall sense today, [unless as I mentioned, it was undeniably clear that God was leading me to do so], is that I would not.

The reason? I'm not sure I want any memories supplanting those of the very special fawns I raised. Selfish? Perhaps. My time with them and theirs with me, may have been brief in the overall scheme of things, but the power of those memories, both the joyous and the sorrowful, and the depth of the connections we had, my fawns and I, I don't think I could suppress enough to do justice to the raising of another one. Even though the sadder memories can still be unexpectedly triggered, I've learned to see them as very small parts of the whole; the happy ones are far more meaningful and numerous, far more vivid, and far outweigh the others. I'd like to keep the memories intact -- in other words, I'd like to leave it at that.

So, there you have it -- the stories of my five little orphan fawns, extraordinary, unforgettable friends, each an individual, each so different, and each possessing the graciousness, gentleness and humility that seem innate in their species, ingrained in their souls. They imparted life lessons to me -- in acceptance and patience, courage and perseverance, trials and triumphs, humor and poise, peace and harmony, activity and repose, hope and trust, loyalty and love. Theirs were lives well lived, borne of natures at once sweet and noble. A toast then -- to Little Lone Fawn, John Doe, Baby Buck, Bambino, and Van Doe. They were an absolute joy to me, these beloved friends. With each one and all of them collectively, I truly knew the pleasure of their company.

If you ever want to talk fawns some more, just stop by my barn -- I'll leave the lights on for you.

Printed in the United States
219730BV00001B/45/P